Mimi Thorisson first captivated readers with *A Kitchen in France*, which displayed her family's idyllic lifestyle in the French countryside and its delectable cuisine. Now that she has found a true home in northern Italy, Mimi shares the sumptuous meals she cooks and eats in her Italian kitchen. The 100 recipes in *A Kitchen in Italy* are Mimi's beloved, family-approved favorites—the staple dishes, perfected over the years, that she returns to again and again.

In the spring, enjoy Mimi's Risi e Bisi, a brothy, risotto-like Venetian dish served in every home and restaurant when peas are in season. There's no better way to use up abundant summer zucchini than in Spaghetti alla Nerano, a dish that encapsulates the beautiful simplicity of Italian cooking. In the fall, turn to a comforting Baked Tagliolini with Prosciutto, a luxurious yet uncomplicated pasta with toasty, salty bites that are beloved by Mimi's kids. When citrus is at its peak in December, pair it with White Chocolate Pistachio Cookies, made with the very best Sicilian pistachios, for a terrific afternoon snack.

With recipes designed for real life but indulgent in flavor, this book will allow you to tuck into a rustic countryside dish on a weeknight or build a special occasion menu to delight your friends. Featuring 150 stunning photographs shot by Mimi's husband, Oddur Thorisson, *A Kitchen in Italy* brings Mimi's Italian secrets to your dinner table.

A KITCHEN *in* ITALY

A KITCHEN *in* ITALY

A YEAR *of*
FAMILY MEALS *and* CELEBRATIONS
from OUR HOME

MIMI THORISSON
Photographs by Oddur Thorisson

CLARKSON POTTER/PUBLISHERS
New York

Clarkson Potter/Publishers
An imprint of the Crown Publishing Group
A division of Penguin Random House LLC
1745 Broadway
New York, NY 10019
clarksonpotter.com
penguinrandomhouse.com

Library of Congress Cataloging-in-Publication Data
Names: Thorisson, Mimi, author. | Thorisson, Oddur, photographer. Title: A kitchen in Italy: a year of family meals and celebrations from our home / Mimi Thorisson; photographs by Oddur Thorisson. Description: New York: Clarkson Potter/Publishers, [2025] | Includes index. |
Identifiers: LCCN 2024057224 (print) | LCCN 2024057225 (ebook) | ISBN 9780593235218 (hardcover) | ISBN 9780593235225 (ebook) Subjects: LCSH: Cooking, Italian. | Seasonal cooking—Italy. | LCGFT: Cookbooks.
Classification: LCC TX723 .T497 2025 (print) | LCC TX723 (ebook) | DDC 641.5945—dc23/eng/20241205
LC record available at https://lccn.loc.gov/2024057224
LC ebook record available at https://lccn.loc.gov/2024057225

ISBN 978-0-593-23521-8
Ebook ISBN 978-0-593-23522-5

Editor: Jennifer Sit | Editorial assistant: Elaine Hennig
Designer: Marysarah Quinn
Production editor: Patricia Shaw
Production: Kim Tyner
Compositor: Merri Ann Morrell
Copy editor: Heather Rodino | Proofreaders: Alissa Fitzgerald, Robin Slutzky, and Sigi Nacson | Indexer: Elizabeth T. Parson
Publicist: Jina Stanfill | Marketer: Andrea Portanova

Manufactured in China

First Edition

The authorized representative in the EU for product safety and compliance is Penguin Random House Ireland, Morrison Chambers, 32 Nassau Street, Dublin D02 YH68, Ireland, https://eu-contact.penguin.ie.

10 9 8 7 6 5 4 3 2 1

For my amazing family

CONTENTS

Painting of Mimi by Italian artist Andrea Ferolla.
Commissioned by her beloved husband for her fiftieth birthday.

INTRODUCTION

In the fall of 2013, I was putting the final touches on my first cookbook, *A Kitchen in France*. It was a huge surprise to find myself, night after night, in that rustic country kitchen in a remote part of France, fine-tuning recipes. I had grown up in bustling Hong Kong, and I had studied finance, so surely my fate was to live in a city and work in an office. And dogs were not exactly part of my plans either, a cat perhaps. Yet here they were, several of them sleeping under the table.

Plus a new child every year, it seemed; an Icelandic husband; and a life so wholly dedicated to food that "spring/summer collection" now meant peas, asparagus, and strawberries rather than shorter hemlines, linens, and flowery prints.

We had left Paris for a bucolic existence in what many describe as a "cul-de-sac" of France. They said we were crazy, but I loved it from the very start. The conversation at lunch was always the same: "What should we do for dinner?" When I was growing up, food was very important to me, but my culinary adventure, one I'm still on, started for real in that farmhouse, cooking for my family. I began sharing my experience on a little blog called *Manger* (that's what people did in those days), and before I knew it, as luck would have it, I was invited to write a cookbook. Another surreal and unexpected twist; sometimes life just happens. The book was an earnest documentation of what it felt like to live in the French countryside, go to markets every day, and cook with seasonal and mostly very local ingredients. It was the life we led and the meals we had together, all photographed by my husband in our home. No sets, no props, no stylist. It was our life, on a page.

A second book, *French Country Cooking*, documented our next chapter in the French countryside, a new home with two kitchens and half the rooms devoted to cooking. It wasn't a restaurant, but with so many children and friends at our table, you could say we were fully booked every night.

We left that life as gently as we fell into it. We wanted to live in Italy, and a third book (or maybe that's just an excuse) opened the door. In *Old World Italian*, I wanted to explore the extraordinary diversity of Italian cuisine, travel the regions, meet locals, and seek advice.

I wanted to find my "cooking legs" in a new territory, build a new home. I wanted to cook like an Italian.

These days I find myself sitting in a fairly rustic kitchen in Italy, a few dogs still under the table. It's a new kitchen in a new apartment here in Torino, where we have now lived for over six years. It's not necessarily that we've come full circle, but writing this book feels in many ways what is often called "back to basics," or a return to my culinary roots. What has always driven me as a home cook is feeding my family, and sometimes dazzling them, when the gods of succulence smile upon me. To host friends, to conjure up simple feasts (and feasts can be simple, especially in Italy, where nothing is simple but the food).

In *A Kitchen in France,* I wanted to share my life and communicate what it's like to take a step back from the roar of the city, to live a simplified life of reduced complications but often heightened pleasures. A life where Mommy bringing home foraged mushrooms is the highlight of the day or when someone cycles to the chicken farm to fetch those delicious sausages we all loved so much.

In this book, I'm back in a city, though Torino does have the charm of a much smaller town and a closeness to nature I have never experienced in a city this size. I hope to demonstrate that you don't have to leave it all behind for a better quality of life. Life is what you make it. What we eat is important. Time spent with family is even more important. Taking the time, every day, to cook something delicious, healthy, and thoughtful is possible. A perfect toast on a Sunday can be a revelation. A good broth can be the best food you ever had (and broth, by the way, is just a bunch of vegetables and often meat that's left simmering while you tend to other things).

Many, though not all, of the recipes in this book are dishes I have discovered since we moved here over six years ago. These are recipes that have found their way into our daily lives and our hearts. Some you will not really find in restaurants or, if you do, only locally. It was a pleasure to discover that even if we are now surrounded by delicious restaurants, I cook as much as ever at home. Yes, a night out is really fun. We love good restaurants, and ordering a pizza is perfect when we're tired or have little time. But there are few greater pleasures than buying simple and good ingredients and cooking a beautiful meal from scratch.

Italians eat very seasonally, at least as much as they do in France, and that's how I've organized the book here. We have vegetable markets in every neighborhood and butchers on every corner. Everyone eats porcini mushrooms and pumpkin soups in the fall, they treat themselves to truffles during the festive season, and during the week we spend in Venice every winter, it seems that there's hardly a dish that doesn't have the delicious local radicchio in the recipe. If you go back in summer, there's no radicchio in anything. The same goes for asparagus and peas in the spring—they're everyday food for most people until the season is over, and then they won't have them again until next year. One of the more embarrassing things you can do here in Italy, at least foodwise, is ask your greengrocer if he's got something that is most likely out of season even if you know it's a long shot. He will shake his head at the ignorance, and when you try to make it better by explaining in your rustic Italian that you actually knew he wouldn't have it, he will still wag his finger. "Next year," he will say, then he will lift up something that has just arrived and say, "Try this, it's a marvel."

The recipes in this book are approved by my family; I've been tweaking and testing most of them for years. The reason they are in this book is because they've passed the test, and that test is simply that I cook them over and over again. There is demand for this food in my house. There are the universally beloved dishes, like meatballs and spaghetti, that everyone likes. But each kid has a dish or two outside that roster that they particularly love. There is something beautiful about a child asking for a favorite dish, especially if it's unusual and healthy. I can never say no to that.

In this crazy world, the sentence "I don't have time to cook" is perfectly understandable. But it can be done. And more important, it can be enjoyed, so very much. My accountant, Claudio, says it best, bless him: "I work all day at a desk, looking at numbers." Then he smiles and continues, "At night when I come home, I want to forget about the numbers and do something with my hands. That's why I love cooking."

This is my kitchen in Italy—now let's cook something good together.

Primavera / Spring

INSALATA PROCIDANA

Lemon Salad, Procida Style

Lemons feature heavily in the cooking of the South, where they have long been plentiful. Lemon pastas, fish cooked with lemons, and so forth. In Procida, the dreamy little island where we have spent our summers for the last few years, they are very proud of their extremely large (you could call them oversize) but not particularly juicy lemons. The Procida lemons are at their prime from late winter until early summer, and diehard natives refuse to use any other lemons for this salad, their best known. The salad in its purest form is of course best enjoyed on location with Procida lemons, but any thick-skinned, fleshy lemon will make for a decent substitute. For an enhanced flavor, consider including finely chopped garlic.

I enjoy offering this salad to my guests who have never had it before, and the reaction is always the same. They are skeptical at first because people are accustomed to using the lemon juice or zest in cooking, but eating the whole lemon? Then intrigue sets in, and finally bliss.

2 pounds / 1 kg Procida lemons (or Meyer lemons)

Extra-virgin olive oil, for serving

A bunch of fresh mint, leaves picked and gently chopped

Flaky sea salt

SERVES 4

1. Peel the lemons, reserving as much of the pith as possible. Quarter the lemons lengthwise, then slice crosswise into bite-size wedges.

2. Place the cut lemons into a mixing bowl and drizzle generously with olive oil. Reserving a few mint leaves for garnish, add the mint, chili flakes, and salt, and toss before serving.

TORTINO DI CARCIOFI

Artichoke Omelet

If I was asked to name a few staples that I couldn't do without in my kitchen, eggs would be high on my list, just after butter. They are so easy to store and so versatile when it comes to whipping up something quick. We most often have eggs for breakfasts, but this artichoke omelet is ideal when you have a need for an improvised yet elegant lunch. It's a complete meal on its own and a great way to use all those beautiful artichokes you simply can't resist buying during your trips to the market.

I find that many people are a little intimidated by artichokes as they can admittedly be a little prickly, literally. But once you've moved past that fear and gotten the hang of preparing them, you'll find they are as easy to work with as any other vegetable.

- 8 small artichokes (about 7 ounces / 200 g each)
- Juice of 1 lemon
- 3 tablespoons extra-virgin olive oil
- 1 garlic clove, gently crushed and peeled
- 6 ounces / 180 ml hot water
- Fine sea salt and freshly ground black pepper
- 4 large eggs
- ½ cup / 50 g grated Parmigiano Reggiano cheese
- ¾ cup / 170 ml whole milk
- A small handful of chopped fresh mint
- A small handful of chopped fresh parsley

SERVES 4

1. Clean the artichokes by removing the outer leaves and any inner choke, then quarter the hearts and soak them in a mixture of water and the lemon juice. Just before using, pat them dry with paper towels.

2. In a medium nonstick skillet, heat 1 tablespoon of the olive oil over medium heat. Add the garlic and sauté until browned, 2 to 3 minutes. Add the artichokes and cook until golden, about 5 minutes. Add the hot water and cook until it has evaporated. Discard the garlic, then season with salt and pepper. Set aside and let cool for a few minutes, reserving the pan.

3. Once the artichokes have cooled, in a medium bowl, beat together the eggs, Parmigiano Reggiano, milk, and an extra pinch of salt to taste. Reserving some of the herbs for garnish, add the mint and parsley, then stir in the cooled artichokes.

4. Heat the remaining 2 tablespoons olive oil in the nonstick skillet over high heat. When the pan is very hot, pour in the egg mixture. Using a spatula, gently pull the egg mixture away from the edges of the pan, then cook, tilting the pan in a circular motion until the eggs have puffed up and cooked through, about 3 minutes. Scatter the remaining herbs over the top and serve immediately.

CASATIELLO

Stuffed Easter Bread

This crusty Neapolitan bread is filled with savory goodness: it's cheesy from the pecorino and provola and salty from the cured meats. A Casatiello is comparable to pane Napoletano, but it's richer, with a more elaborate filling, and is traditionally shaped like a doughnut. Some versions, like this one, include placing four eggs at the top of the bread, each held by a string of the dough. The eggs and the shape of the Casatiello represent the cross that Christ died on, and the crown of thorns. Traditionally Neapolitans made the bread only at Easter, but the pastiera napoletana, the famous Easter cake, can now be found year-round, if you're lucky.

The first time we had this bread was on a trip to Procida with friends. Oddur, my husband, had taken a morning walk and stumbled upon a small gastronomia (deli) where they were selling traditional, local food. Many people were ahead of him in the queue, and when it was his turn, there was only one large slice left, the end part. I remember him walking into the hotel garden, holding the bread with two hands as if he had discovered a treasure. And a treasure it was: The following morning we were back early, this time at the front of the queue.

Dough

1¼ cups / 300 ml lukewarm water

2¼ teaspoons active dry yeast (or 1 packet active dry yeast)

2 tablespoons / 25 g lard, plus more for greasing

1 teaspoon granulated sugar

3½ tablespoons / 50 ml extra-virgin olive oil, plus more for drizzling

1 tablespoon freshly ground black pepper

4⅓ cups / 550 g all-purpose flour, plus more for dusting

1 teaspoon fine sea salt

Filling

5 ounces / 150 g Neapolitan salami, diced

4 ounces / 125 g prosciutto cotto or ham, diced

4 ounces / 125 g Pecorino Romano cheese, grated

4 ounces / 125 g provola cheese, diced

4 large eggs

SERVES 6

1. **Make the dough.** Pour the lukewarm water into a small bowl. Whisk in the yeast until dissolved. Let the yeast activate until frothy, 5 to 10 minutes.

2. In a large bowl, combine the activated yeast mixture, lard, sugar, olive oil, and pepper. Slowly incorporate the flour and combine with a fork. When the dough begins to come together, add the salt and knead until the dough is smooth and elastic, about 10 minutes.

3. Transfer the dough to a floured work surface and shape it into a ball. Cut an X into the top of the dough. Cover with plastic wrap and let rise in a bowl in a warm place for about 1½ hours, or until doubled in size.

4. When ready to roll, cut off a piece of dough (about 2.8 ounces / 80 g). Roll out the remaining dough into a 12 × 16-inch / 30 × 40 cm rectangle (about ½ inch / 1.25 cm thick) with a rolling pin.

recipe continues »

Casatiello CONTINUED

5. **Assemble the filling.** Drizzle the rolled-out dough with olive oil and scatter with the salami, prosciutto, pecorino, and provola cheese. Starting from the long side of the rectangle, roll the dough tightly into a log.

6. Grease a 9½-inch / 24 cm ring mold or Bundt pan with lard. Place the dough into the mold, joining the ends to form a ring. Press the dough down gently to flatten it slightly. Using the back of a spoon, create four small indentations in the top of the dough ring. Place one egg into each indentation.

7. Divide the reserved dough into 8 even pieces. Roll each piece into a thin strip. Place 2 strips over each egg in a crisscross pattern and press gently to seal. Cover loosely with plastic wrap and let it rise in a warm place for about 1½ hours, until risen to the rim.

8. Preheat the oven to 350°F / 180°C.

9. Grease the surface of the casatiello with more lard. Bake until golden brown and fully cooked, 1 hour. Let cool in the pan for 10 minutes before unmolding. Slice around the eggs and serve warm.

CHICKPEA FARINATA

This slightly crispy, crepe-like creation is ideal party food. It goes beautifully with a nice sparkling wine, and it appeases the palate while you wait for more substantial things. Farinatas are very prevalent in Torino, where we live, but they come originally, I believe, from the coastline—Liguria here in Italy, but the tradition stretches westward to France.

When we host dinner parties, and we do often, we like to open some bubbles for our guests the moment they arrive, followed by a steady stream of fresh-out-of-the-oven farinatas cut into slices. The demand never ceases, so it's important to know when to stop and continue with dinner—you've got to leave them wanting more.

2 cups / 250 g chickpea flour

¼ cup / 60 ml extra-virgin olive oil, plus more for greasing the pan

1½ teaspoons fine sea salt

Freshly ground black pepper

SERVES 4

1. Place the chickpea flour in a large bowl. Slowly whisk in 2⅔ cups / 650 ml water until no lumps remain. Stir in the olive oil and salt until smooth. Cover with a lid or plastic wrap and set aside for at least 4 hours in the coolest part of the kitchen, or up to overnight in the refrigerator.

2. Preheat the oven to 400°F / 200°C and generously grease a 14-inch / 35 cm diameter round pan with olive oil.

3. Pour the batter into the prepared pan. Bake until a golden crust forms, about 20 minutes.

4. Sprinkle the farinata with pepper. Slice into 6 to 8 pieces and serve immediately.

A Life in Food

As long as I can remember, I have been fascinated by food. One reason is that I grew up in Hong Kong, where obsessing over food is normal. In that sense, you could say my father was a normal guy, only more so. As a little girl I was stick thin and sprouty, and this upset my father greatly. He wanted me to be healthy, and he also didn't want me to look underfed; he felt it reflected badly on him in front of his friends. So he curbed his frustrations, and instead of forcing me to eat what I didn't like (well, he tried that first), he took me on Wednesday afternoons to satisfy my palate. One of our regular haunts on evenings like that would be a stop for tripes, sold by an old man at the side of a road. Looking back at my childhood in Hong Kong, I recall a delectable blur of endless banquets and feasts, of tables swaying from too much food, memories of the in-between snacks that my father cheekily could never resist and for which I was his partner in crime. My father, Louis, is gone now, but that's how I'll always remember him, sneaking in a snack between meals.

In France, every summer, I would spend my time in the kitchens of my aunt and my grandmother, watching them perform what to me at the time was nothing less than pure alchemy (my favorite was my aunt Francine's stuffed tomatoes, Provençal style). I was fascinated by my cousin Stefane's drum set, by the posters in his room, and by how cool his friends were (they all smoked, of course), but the stove had an even greater allure, and that's what I watched instead of TV. Every day at lunch, my grandmother would have meat or fish, but dinner was always the same, a simple potage of legumes. Our treat together was to boil a large artichoke when we were alone in the kitchen, then we'd sit down, dip the meaty part of the leaves in vinaigrette, and talk about life and recipes. But mostly recipes.

Back home in Hong Kong, I would regularly invite my whole class to my father's club for after-school meals. Another food obsessive, Jimmy Chan, and I took turns. We usually ordered everything on the menu, all the club food we loved—clam chowder, club sandwiches, and chicken waffles, with ice cream to finish. When he would get the bill, my father would call my name from his office, the roar reverberating through the house. But he always forgave me—he understood.

Later, when I studied in France and England, I fell hard for the food scene in both places. In London, it was the budding gastropubs in the '90s, late nights drinking beer, listening to indie bands, and munching on steak and kidney pie. It was in Paris that I started cooking. I was just as mesmerized by music and fashion (oh boy, the fashion) as all my friends, but I may have been the only one who experimented with making soufflés in my spare time, not always with the best results (you have to start somewhere). I remember sitting in Parisian bistros, at about eighteen years old, in my vintage smoking jacket and jeans, eating steak tartare and enjoying "un ballon de rouge," feeling like such a grown-up, yet I was still such a kid.

My husband, Oddur, is in love with restaurants, to the point that I've never met anyone like him in that regard. Pair two people like us, and our first years together were a furious hunt for the best restaurant wherever we went. Meticulous research, countless lunches and dinners of varying quality, but in the end it didn't matter because the result was always the same: the two of us opposite each other, enjoying a meal.

For a while, that was our job, going to restaurants in Paris, every day. That's also when the lines started to blur. My relationship with food has always been a romantic one. Never practical. No particular structure. After I started writing cookbooks, I could no longer deny that food was now also my job. They say it's dangerous to marry your lover, or as Wordsworth wrote, "We murder to dissect."

Does a passion die when it also becomes work?

I have found, happily, that it does not. I am older now, wiser, and more experienced. The more I learn about food, the more I like it. The eighteen-year-old me was blissfully ignorant; she didn't know that the "best steak tartare" in the world was, in fact, not. She didn't know how to cook for forty people. She didn't know how to stir up a great dinner for a whole family after a difficult day. And she didn't know that basil is different in Liguria and Campania.

It gives me great joy to discover new flavors and techniques. Knowing things is beautiful. When I make a simple pasta dish, it gives me pleasure to know how it came to be, to think of all the nonnas who made it before me and why they always made it this way. It gives me great pleasure to know that in hundreds of thousands of kitchens across the globe, in various languages, people are looking at the spattered pages of my cookbooks while they are sipping wine, stirring pots, and chopping onions, waiting for their friends to arrive, their date to show up, or the kids to come to the table.

We might be married now, food and I, but I'm still in love.

SAUTÉ DI VONGOLE E COZZE

Sautéed Mussels & Clams

Mussels are, in my mind at least, always connected to the very Belgian or northern French dish of moules marinières with French fries. Vongole, or clams, on the other hand, are inextricably linked in my head to one of Italy's favorite pasta dishes, spaghetti alle vongole. This simple dish is a way of bringing these delicious and healthy mollusks together in one bubbling pan. The potential benefits are endless, but let me list a few: This is a wonderful way to start a beautiful meal; a shared plate and a great bottle of crisp wine will light up a table like few dishes can. It's lighter for those who are concerned about that (and we all are sometimes), but if you are not concerned, then the broth is ideal for dipping in a good slice or two of bread. Finally, now that you've had your dose of seafood flavors, you can go anywhere you like with the primi.

Fine sea salt and freshly ground black pepper

2¼ pounds / 1 kg clams, such as vongole veraci

2¼ pounds / 1 kg mussels

A loaf of ciabatta bread, sliced into 8 pieces

5 tablespoons / 80 ml extra-virgin olive oil, plus more for drizzling

1 garlic clove, thinly sliced

One 1-inch/ 2.5 cm piece of ginger, peeled and finely grated

1½ cups / 360 ml dry white wine

SERVES 4

1. Fill a large bowl with lightly salted water and add the clams. Let stand for at least 1 hour to eliminate the sand. Drain the clams, then rinse the clams and mussels several times until there is no more sand. Scrub if necessary.

2. Preheat the broiler. Arrange the bread slices on a baking sheet and drizzle with olive oil. Broil until golden brown, 2 to 4 minutes.

3. Heat a large sauté pan over high heat and add the olive oil. Add the garlic and ginger and cook until golden, about 2 minutes. Add the mussels and clams, give the pan a good shake, and add the wine. Cover and cook, stirring occasionally, until all the clams and mussels have opened, up to 7 minutes. Do not overcook them or they will be chewy and lose their taste.

4. Season with pepper and serve immediately along with the broth and with the toasted ciabatta.

CLEAR SPRING SOUP *with* PEAS & ARTICHOKES À LA EUROPEO MATTOZZI

The thought of Naples brings to mind pastas in red sauces, the freshest seafood, sweet breakfasts (sfogliatelle), and great coffee. And pizzas, obviously. My own personal and Proustian food remembrance that takes me back to this wild and beautiful city by the bay is this simple, almost peasant-like clear soup filled with most of the good things spring has to offer. And not just back to Naples, back to a specific, gorgeous evening at the beloved restaurant Europeo Mattozzi. It's been one of our favorite spots in Italy for years. The room is lovely, and the food is consistently outstanding in a seasonal, old-fashioned, and homey kind of way. Most important, the people—not least the charmer of a host, Alfonso—make the place a home away from home. I would make the trip (six hours by train from Torino) just to give him a hug and have this soup.

4 tablespoons / 60 ml extra-virgin olive oil, plus more for drizzling

1 spring onion, finely chopped

2 medium potatoes, peeled and cut into small dice

1 cup / 150 g shelled fava beans, blanched and peeled

1 cup / 150 g green peas, fresh or frozen

Fine sea salt and freshly ground black pepper

4 cups / 950 ml vegetable stock

2 garlic cloves, minced

2 artichokes, cleaned and hearts cut into matchsticks

A bunch of fresh basil, chopped

A bunch of fresh mint, chopped

A handful of mixed fresh herbs (such as parsley, thyme, and chives), finely chopped

½ cup / 50 g grated Parmigiano Reggiano cheese

Grated zest of 1 lemon, for garnish

SERVES 4

1. In a large pot, heat 2 tablespoons of the olive oil over medium heat. Add the spring onion and sauté until translucent and lightly golden, about 3 minutes.

2. Add the potatoes, fava beans, and peas to the pot. Season with a pinch of salt and pepper. Continue to sauté until softened, stirring occasionally, about 5 minutes.

3. Pour in the vegetable stock and bring to a boil. Reduce the heat to low and simmer until the vegetables are tender, 15 to 20 minutes.

4. In a medium sauté pan, heat the remaining 2 tablespoons olive oil over medium heat. Add the garlic and sauté until fragrant, about 1 minute. Add the artichokes and cook until beginning to soften, 5 to 7 minutes. If needed, add a splash of water to prevent sticking. Season with salt and pepper and set aside.

5. Once the vegetables in the broth are tender, stir in the herbs until well combined. Adjust the seasoning if necessary.

6. Serve with the sautéed artichokes, Parmigiano Reggiano, lemon zest, and a drizzle of olive oil.

RISI E BISI

Venetian Rice & Peas

Rice and peas, as this dish is colloquially known, is one of the most traditional dishes of Veneto, served in every home and restaurant when peas are in season. Like many risottos, this is a recipe that's hearty and light at the same time, fresh yet filling. Many versions exist; such is the nature of long-established dishes. Some are closer to a classic risotto in their creamy consistency, while others take on a soupier texture. What Venetians seem to agree on, regardless of the consistency, is that risi e bisi is not technically a risotto; it's simply risi e bisi.

I like mine on the soupier side, full of the most flavorful peas, and as tradition dictates, I enjoy mine with a spoon rather than a fork. It's one of my favorite things to order in restaurants. Just saying it aloud brings about a measure of childlike happiness.

1½ quarts / liters vegetable stock

1⅔ cups / 250 g green peas, fresh or frozen

Fine sea salt and freshly ground black pepper

¼ cup / 60 ml extra-virgin olive oil

⅓ cup / 50 g finely chopped onion (about ½ small onion)

¼ cup / 30 g finely chopped bacon

1¾ cups / 350 g Vialone Nano or Arborio rice

4 tablespoons / 60 g salted butter

½ cup / 50 g grated Parmigiano Reggiano cheese

3 sprigs of fresh parsley, finely chopped

SERVES 4

1. In a large saucepan, combine the stock and ⅔ cup / 100 g of the peas. Bring to a boil and cook until al dente, about 5 minutes. Drain with a slotted spoon and transfer to a large bowl. Add a ladle of the hot broth and blend with an immersion blender until smooth. Season with salt to taste and set aside.

2. In a medium sauté pan, combine the olive oil, onion, and bacon. Cook over low heat until golden, about 10 minutes.

3. Increase the heat to medium. Add the rice and sauté, about 1 minute, until well coated. Add a ladle of the hot broth. When the liquid is mostly absorbed, add another ladle of broth, stirring constantly and adding more once each addition is absorbed to keep the rice covered at all times. Repeat this process until the rice is cooked through but still al dente, 17 to 19 minutes. In the last 5 minutes of cooking, add the remaining 1 cup / 150 g peas and continue cooking. Remove the risotto from heat.

4. Stir in the blended peas, butter, and Parmigiano Reggiano until the mixture is creamy and well combined. Season with salt and pepper.

5. Sprinkle with parsley and serve.

A MAIN LIBRE
DESSIN A MAIN LIBRE
CHAMPAGNE
Pol Roger

MACCO DI FAVE

Thick Sicilian Fava Bean Soup

Fava beans are one of my favorite vegetables because they lend such flavor to any dish and, despite their humble origins, also a measure of elegance.

In Sicily, where this recipe originates, they often use dried fava beans, as we do here, in place of the fresh ones. So this soup is as good an example as any in the canon of Italian cuisine of how a lowly peasant dish born out of necessity or what was available has today been elevated to the highest tables and considered nothing less than "gourmet."

1 pound / 450 g dried fava beans, soaked overnight

A bunch of wild fennel, bulbs chopped and fronds reserved

¼ cup / 60 ml extra-virgin olive oil

1 onion, finely diced

2 carrots, finely diced

1 celery rib, finely diced

Fine sea salt and freshly ground black pepper

SERVES 4 TO 6

1. Place the soaked beans in a large stockpot. Cover with water and add the fennel fronds. Bring to a boil over medium heat, skimming off the foam with a slotted spoon. Reduce the heat to low. Cook until the beans are tender, 2 to 3 hours. Drain and reserve the bean water.

2. Once the beans are done, in a large pot, heat the olive oil over low heat. Add the onion, carrots, celery, and fennel. Season with pepper. Sauté until golden, about 5 minutes.

3. Add the drained beans to the pot and cook until simmering, about 2 minutes. Add the reserved bean water and salt and cook until the consistency is creamy, about 1 hour.

TIMBALLO DI CAPELLI D'ANGELO

There is something magical about a dish made from relatively humble ingredients yet one that arrives at the table with such a sense of occasion. This timballo is one of those treasures, a dish that feels like a secret shared between generations. Angel hair pasta, fresh peas, sautéed zucchini, and a rich, creamy béchamel, all bound together in a glorious golden bowl, a pasta nest, gently turned upside down, that's as beautiful as it is comforting.

I love how this dish, with an air of nostalgic charm, brings the spirit of old-fashioned cooking into a modern kitchen. A labor of love and a thing of beauty, delicate layers that carry a surprise of flavors, perfect for celebrating spring when everything seems to be humming with promise and possibility.

It's my favorite spring offering.

5 tablespoons / 70 g salted butter, plus more for greasing the pan

3 tablespoons extra-virgin olive oil

2 spring onions, finely chopped

3½ ounces / 100 g mortadella, cubed

7 ounces / 200 g fresh peas

3½ ounces / 100 g sliced zucchini rounds

14 ounces / 400 g dried angel hair pasta

Fine sea salt and freshly ground black pepper

½ cup / 50 g dried breadcrumbs

5 ounces / 150 g caciocavallo or provola cheese, diced

5 ounces / 150 g fresh mozzarella cheese, diced

3½ ounces / 100 g grated Parmigiano Reggiano cheese

14 ounces / 400 ml Béchamel (page 98)

SERVES 4

1. Preheat the oven to 350°F / 180°C. Grease a 9½-inch / 24 cm (2.5-liter capacity) tube springform pan or timballo mold with butter.

2. Bring a large pot of salted water to a boil over high heat.

3. In a medium sauté pan, heat 3 tablespoons of the butter and 1 tablespoon of the olive oil over medium heat until the butter melts. Add the spring onions and sauté until softened, about 3 minutes. Add the mortadella, peas, and zucchini and sauté until golden brown, about 3 more minutes.

4. Once the water is boiling, add the pasta and undercook it by 1 minute according to the package directions.

5. Drain the pasta and place it in a large bowl. Immediately toss with the remaining 2 tablespoons olive oil. Season with salt and pepper.

6. Sprinkle the prepared mold with the breadcrumbs. Add half of the pasta to the prepared pan. Scatter the caciocavallo and mozzarella over the top, then add the vegetable mixture in an even layer. Sprinkle with half of the Parmigiano Reggiano and cover with half of the béchamel sauce. Top with the remaining pasta, Parmigiano Reggiano, and béchamel. Cut the remaining 2 tablespoons butter into small pieces and scatter on top.

7. Bake until golden, about 25 minutes. Let cool for 5 minutes. Gently unmold upside down onto a serving plate. Cut into slices and serve.

SPAGHETTI AGLIO E OLIO

You could say this is spaghetti in its purest form, the pasta equivalent of buttered toast. Most pasta sauces will demand your attention: A well-made ragù will hit you in the heart. A sugo made from perfectly ripe tomatoes will make you think only of the tomatoes; it will make you dream of the tomatoes. The pasta becomes a canvas, or a conduit, for more expressive ingredients. Even mediocre-quality dried pasta can taste pretty good once lathered in the right sauce.

Not this recipe. Here, the spaghetti is the soprano, which is why you must try to use good-quality pasta; here, you invest in the spaghetti. This means the pasta you use should probably be Italian, hopefully from Gragnano, near Naples, where dried pasta stems from and is still its spiritual home. Really good olive oil will make this dish sing, too. And to continue the musical analogy, this may be an acoustic type of dish, but you can adjust the volume to your taste depending on how much garlic or chili you add. Some like the subtlety of the garlic-infused oil; others like it spicy. Making this recipe is simple enough, but to perfect it takes a bit of practice. Once it's perfected (*al dente* is the key phrase here), you are ready to take on any sauce next because you've mastered the basics, and so much of what comes next traces back to this dish. It's about knowing what pasta can and should taste and feel like, and this dish reveals that.

½ cup / 120 ml extra-virgin olive oil

8 garlic cloves, thinly sliced

2 teaspoons crushed red pepper flakes, or 1 tablespoon chopped fresh chile pepper

1 pound / 500 g dried spaghetti

Fine sea salt and freshly ground black pepper

⅓ cup / 50 g chopped fresh parsley

2 tablespoons grated Parmigiano Reggiano cheese

SERVES 4 TO 6

1. Bring a large pot of salted water to a boil over high heat.

2. In a large sauté pan, heat the olive oil over medium heat. Add the garlic and cook until golden, 2 to 3 minutes. Add the pepper flakes and cook for about 1 minute, then remove the pan from the heat.

3. Meanwhile, add the spaghetti to the boiling water and cook to al dente according to the package directions. Reserving 1 cup / 250 ml of the pasta water, drain the pasta.

4. Add the drained pasta to the pan with the garlic oil along with ¾ cup/ 175 ml of the reserved pasta water. Toss to combine and raise the heat to high, giving the pasta a good stir until you see the sauce thickening slightly, about 2 minutes. Add the rest of the pasta water if it evaporates too fast. Remove from the heat.

5. To serve, season with salt and pepper and garnish with the parsley and Parmigiano Reggiano.

RISOTTO *with* MOUNTAIN HERBS

Take any rudimentary dish, say boiled fish and potatoes, sprinkle or cook with the right herbs (which can often be any herbs), and you get an instant elevation of flavors. I've always cooked with all sorts of herbs. Before we lived in the countryside and grew our own (we still do on our terrace here in Torino), I used to have little ziplocks of assorted herbs in our fridge in Paris—they were my little treasures. In northern Italy, where risottos are most prevalent, it is very common to make this twist on the basic risotto with parmigiano and whatever herbs are available—it's a good example of how you can make something refined and delicious out of simple, even humble, ingredients.

1. In a large saucepan, bring the stock to a simmer over medium-high heat. Reduce the heat to low to keep the stock at a simmer.

2. In a medium sauté pan, heat the olive oil over medium heat. Add the shallots and sauté until softened but not golden, about 4 minutes. Add the rice and cook, stirring, until the rice is evenly coated. Add the wine and deglaze the pan, stirring constantly, until reduced by half, about 3 minutes.

3. Add a ladle of the hot stock and gently stir. When the liquid is mostly absorbed, add another ladle of stock, stirring constantly and adding more to keep the rice covered at all times. Repeat this process until the rice is creamy but still al dente, 15 to 17 minutes.

4. In a small bowl, combine the melted butter and herbs.

5. Add the herb butter, Parmigiano Reggiano, and lemon juice to the risotto, stirring vigorously to make it creamier. Remove the pan from the heat and let rest for about 2 minutes, then serve.

1½ quarts / liters chicken or vegetable stock

5 tablespoons / 75 ml extra-virgin olive oil

3 shallots, finely diced

2 cups / 400 g carnaroli rice

⅓ cup / 80 ml dry white wine

3 tablespoons / 45 g salted butter, melted and kept warm

A handful of fresh seasonal herbs (like rosemary, sage, marjoram, and thyme), finely chopped

⅔ cup / 60 g grated Parmigiano Reggiano cheese

A squeeze of fresh lemon juice

SERVES 4

RISOTTO *with* ASPARAGUS & LEMON

I'm always amazed at how wonderfully nature tends to our needs and gives us the perfect food for each part of the year. All we have to do is follow her lead, follow the seasons. After the rich food of winter—the stews filled with root vegetables, the gratins, the sumptuous dishes of pasta and beans—come the more refreshing, yet nourishing, vegetables of spring. First to arrive are the artichokes and not long after, the asparagus. We are happy to start to blanch a few as a starter or a side dish, dressed with a little olive oil and lemon. Sometimes we get a bit more creative with the dressing, add some finely chopped hard-boiled eggs or a fried egg on top. Soon after, someone requests this risotto. It's so flavorful, and the lemon zest gives it that extra springy freshness. I can't think of a better, more elegant spring lunch.

1½ quarts / liters chicken or vegetable stock

3 tablespoons extra-virgin olive oil, plus more for garnish

1 medium onion, finely diced

Grated zest and juice of 1 lemon

2 fresh sage leaves

14 ounces / 400 g asparagus, ends trimmed, tips reserved, and stalks sliced into 1-inch / 2.5 cm pieces

2 cups / 400 g Arborio rice

3 tablespoons / 45 g salted butter

⅔ cup / 60 g grated Parmigiano Reggiano cheese

Fine sea salt and freshly ground black pepper

SERVES 4 TO 6

1. In a large saucepan, bring the stock to a simmer over medium-high heat. Reduce the heat to low to keep the stock at a simmer.

2. In a medium sauté pan, heat 2 tablespoons of the olive oil over medium heat. Add the onion, half of the lemon zest, and the sage leaves and sauté until translucent and fragrant, about 4 minutes. Add the sliced asparagus and enough of the hot stock to cover. Cover and cook until the asparagus is tender, 3 minutes. Remove the sage leaves.

3. Remove half of the asparagus with a slotted spoon and add it to a blender along with some of the stock. Blend until smooth and saucy.

4. Add the remaining tablespoon of olive oil to the pan and heat over medium heat. Add the rice and stir well to coat. Add the lemon juice and stir until absorbed.

5. Add a ladle of hot stock and gently stir. When the liquid is mostly absorbed, add another ladle of stock, stirring constantly and adding more once each addition is absorbed to keep the rice covered at all times. Repeat this process until the rice is creamy, about 10 minutes. Stir in the reserved asparagus tips and continue cooking, adding stock and stirring, until the rice is creamy but still al dente, about 2 minutes. Stir in the blended asparagus and cook until heated through, 1 minute more.

6. Remove the pan from the heat. Add the butter and Parmigiano Reggiano, stirring vigorously to make the risotto creamier.

7. Garnish with a drizzle of olive oil, salt, pepper, and the remaining lemon zest. Serve immediately.

FAVA BEAN & SALMON CAKES

I've always been a huge fan of what I like to categorize as "clubhouse food." Food that is often served by the side of a swimming pool or at least with a view of a pool, somehow. I'm thinking of easy-to-serve, tasty, crunchy, and salty dishes—food that everyone likes, a close cousin of elevated picnic food. I had variations of fish cakes all the time growing up, at my parents' club in Hong Kong, and a type of fish cake—I can't remember which—was one of the first things I learned to make, ages ago. I've been making fish cakes ever since, all sorts and made of any fish, often with potatoes and fresh herbs, and generously accompanied by rich sauces, aioli, or tartar. I've had fish cakes (or polpette di pesce, as they often call them here) in various parts of Italy, most notably in Sicily, where they predictably like to squeeze a bit of lemon on top.

I'm including fava beans in this recipe, which I must admit I haven't had anywhere in Italy, but I love pan-fried fava beans as a side dish, and I think this is a marriage that will last. One of the other reasons we love them so much is how relatively short the season is. Compared to carrots or potatoes, which are always there for you, there is something extra special about fresh fava beans due to their fleeting nature. Not to mention all the hard work that goes into peeling them (two layers, no less), but luckily we have many small hands to help us, and when those are gone, we will, I suppose, have more time to do it ourselves.

10 ounces / 300 g waxy potatoes, peeled and diced

10 ounces / 300 g salmon, cooked and flaked (skin removed)

½ cup plus 2 tablespoons / 80 g chopped fresh dill, plus more for garnish

Grated zest of 1 lemon, plus more for garnish

6 tablespoons / 45 g dried breadcrumbs

4 cups / 300 g shelled fava beans, blanched and peeled

½ teaspoon crushed red pepper flakes, plus more for garnish

Fine sea salt and freshly ground black pepper

1 large egg

3 tablespoons all-purpose flour, for dredging

¼ cup / 60 ml extra-virgin olive oil

¾ cup / 180 ml mayonnaise

MAKES 12 CAKES

1. Place the potatoes in a large pot of salted water. Bring to a boil over medium-high heat and cook until very tender, about 20 minutes. Drain, then mash.

2. In a large bowl, combine the mashed potatoes, flaked salmon, dill, lemon zest, breadcrumbs, fava beans, pepper flakes, salt, and pepper. Then add the egg. Shape into 12 patties about 3 inches / 7.5 cm in diameter. Refrigerate for about 20 minutes.

3. Place the flour in a shallow bowl and dredge the fish cakes in the flour.

4. In a large skillet, heat the olive oil over medium heat. Add the fish cakes in batches and cook until golden brown, 3 to 4 minutes on each side.

5. For the sauce, in a medium bowl, combine the mayonnaise with a sprinkle of dill, a teaspoon of lemon zest, and red pepper flakes to taste. Mix well and serve alongside the salmon cakes.

CASSUOLA NAPOLETANA

Neapolitan Fish Stew

For the last few years, we have spent the first days of May in Naples. Work brings us there, but just being in Naples is a reward in itself, and this little week has become one of the highlights of our gastronomic calendar. Campania is of course the region of tomatoes and seafood, and this is a very traditional, old-fashioned, local fish stew full of both. Italian food is family food, and even if you have cassuola in restaurants, it still feels like home cooking, which I love.

We regularly make this dish at home. It's much easier than you'd think, and in many ways, it's comparable to a spaghetti puttanesca (here the pasta is swapped for fish). Most of the ingredients are probably already lurking in your cupboards and drawers—it's one of those extremely comforting pantry dishes that we sometimes like to say is "made out of nothing." And what a sweet nothing this is.

2¼ pounds / 1 kg monkfish or any firm-fleshed fish fillets

2 tablespoons extra-virgin olive oil

1 garlic clove, thinly sliced

1⅓ pounds / 600 g canned peeled tomatoes, chopped

16 black olives, pitted

1 tablespoon capers, rinsed

Fine sea salt and freshly ground black pepper

A bunch of fresh parsley, chopped

SERVES 4

NOTE

If you like it spicy, you can add crushed red pepper flakes or chopped chile pepper along with the garlic.

1. Gently wash the fish fillets, pat them dry, and set aside on a plate.

2. In a large saucepan, heat the olive oil over medium heat. Add the garlic and sauté until golden, about 2 minutes. Add the tomatoes and cook, undisturbed, until softened, about 15 minutes.

3. Reduce the heat to low. Add the monkfish, olives, and capers and cook until the fish is fully cooked, about 20 minutes. Do not overcook or the fish will fall apart. Taste and season with salt and pepper if necessary.

4. Top with parsley and serve immediately.

CALAMARI FRITTI

Before we lived in Italy, we used to spend most of our holidays here, in rented houses in Tuscany and Umbria, in charming hotels by the sea. Over the years we've gone to countless restaurants, and chances are that somewhere in our order, especially if we are near the sea, is some fried seafood.

My husband and I like to order the fritto misto, a big plate of fried seafood with a squeeze of lemon. We noticed the kids tended to avoid the bony fish and finished all the calamari in seconds. This led us to changing our order, one fritto misto and one fried calamari for the kids, the only way for us adults to get any calamari at all. Since we have this dish so often in restaurants, I somehow never made it at home until one day the kids begged me. Now we have it all the time at home, and it's one of my favorite meals. Everyone gathers around the kitchen table with white wine, fresh salads, and batches of the freshest fried calamari.

2 medium to large squid, cleaned, sliced into ½-inch / 1.2 cm wide pieces, and tentacles separated, about 21 ounces / 600 grams

2 cups / 240 g semolina flour, for dredging

Vegetable oil, for frying

Fine sea salt and freshly ground black pepper

1 lemon, cut into wedges

SERVES 4

1. Pat the squid dry. Place the flour in a shallow bowl and dredge the squid pieces in the flour.

2. Pour 2 inches / 5 cm oil into a large, high-sided pan. Heat the oil to about 325°F / 160°C over medium heat. Working in batches, fry the squid until golden, 3 to 4 minutes. Drain on a plate lined with paper towels. Season with salt and pepper.

3. Serve immediately with lemon wedges on the side.

VEAL SCALLOPINE *with* LEMON

These veal scallops may be one of the very first Italian dishes I made for my young family in Paris all those years ago. It wasn't easy to find a French butcher who agreed to slice the veal this thinly, and after much negotiation, I still ended up with a cut that was, at best, somewhere between an Italian veal scallop and the traditional, thicker French veal cutlet. Living in Italy, I no longer have this problem, though when I buy this Italian staple, the local butchers cutting it to perfection every time, I can't help but smile and remember my Paris days.

Obviously my kids love this dish, and so does my mother-in-law, who likes her meat cooked through. When serving this dish, we alternate between the classics: creamy with mushrooms when they are in season, with Marsala, or breaded, Milanese style. But in spring, when we have the most beautiful lemons in the world at our disposal, from Amalfi or neighboring Liguria, it has to be this version.

1⅓ pounds / 600 g thinly sliced veal loin

Fine sea salt and freshly ground black pepper

All-purpose flour, for dredging

¼ cup / 60 ml extra-virgin olive oil

4 tablespoons / 60 g unsalted butter

2 garlic cloves, peeled and sliced finely

Grated zest and juice of 1½ lemons

1 sprig of fresh parsley, chopped

SERVES 4

1. Cover the veal cutlets with a sheet of parchment paper and pound each with a meat pounder until they are ¼ inch / 6 mm thick. Season with salt and pepper.

2. Place flour in a shallow bowl and dredge the veal cutlets in the flour. Shake off the excess.

3. In a large sauté pan, heat the olive oil over medium heat, then add the butter. When it starts to sizzle, add the garlic and lemon zest to infuse the oil. Add the veal in batches and cook until golden brown, about 1 minute on each side. Add the lemon juice and cook until the juice is reduced slightly, about 1 minute. Discard the garlic cloves. Season with salt and pepper and scatter a little parsley on top.

AGNELLO E PISELLI

Braised Easter Lamb with Peas

This is a typical Easter dish from the region of Campania. It goes along with similar festive dishes like Casatiello (page 23) and pastiera—all the most symbolic specialties of the season. The lamb is browned and then braised with onion until tender. Peas are added to the braise until they, too, are tender. The result would be delicious on its own, but most recipes, like mine, suggest finishing the dish with beaten eggs and freshly grated pecorino and parmigiano cheeses, creating a creamy sauce when heated in the pan.

3 pounds / 1.3 kg lamb shoulder, cut into 1½-inch / 3.8 cm pieces

1½ cups / 375 ml dry white wine

Fine sea salt

Extra-virgin olive oil

1 medium onion, thinly sliced

14 ounces / 400 g fresh peas

2 large eggs

1 ounce / 30 g freshly grated Pecorino Romano cheese

1 ounce / 30 g freshly grated Parmigiano Reggiano cheese

A few sprigs of fresh rosemary, leaves finely chopped

SERVES 4 TO 6

1. Place the lamb in a large bowl with ¾ cup of the wine, just enough cold water to cover, and a generous pinch of salt. Cover and let marinate at room temperature for 40 minutes. Drain and pat dry. Set aside.

2. In a large pot, heat a generous drizzle of olive oil over medium heat. Add the onion and sauté until tender and fragrant, about 4 minutes. Add the lamb to the pot and cook until browned on all sides, about 15 minutes. Add the remaining ¾ cup wine and deglaze the pan, stirring constantly.

3. Reduce the heat to low, cover, and cook until the lamb is almost tender, about 1 hour. Add a little hot water as needed to keep the lamb moist at all times.

4. When the lamb has about 20 minutes left, add the peas and cook until the lamb is fully tender and the flavors have melded.

5. In a small bowl, beat the eggs with the Pecorino Romano, Parmigiano Reggiano, rosemary, and a pinch of salt.

6. Reduce the heat to very low. Add more hot water if the pan is dry, then gently stir in the egg mixture, taking the pan off the heat for a minute. Return to the heat and cook, stirring, until the eggs thicken into a creamy sauce, 2 minutes. Finish with a drizzle of olive oil and serve.

INVOLTINI DI POLLO

Stuffed Chicken in Parmesan Cream Sauce

A lot of Italian dishes could be described as comfort food, such is the heartwarming nature of the cuisine. Some dishes, like this one, go a step further and could almost be described as "kiddie food" for children and adults, too, of course. I typically make this toward the end of the week when the young ones are exhausted from school and various activities and in need of something they truly love. When we designed the kitchen in our new apartment in Torino, it was very important to me that we could all dine together in the kitchen, even though the dining room is nearby. Some food—like this dish—simply tastes better in the kitchen. It's mostly a self-selecting process; we instinctively lay the table in the room where the food feels most at home.

1. Place flour in a shallow bowl and dredge the chicken in the flour. Place each piece of chicken on a slice of prosciutto and divide the mozzarella among them. Season with salt and pepper. Roll them up and secure each with a toothpick.

2. In a large cast-iron skillet, heat the olive oil over medium heat. Add the chicken rolls and cook until browned, 5 minutes per side.

3. Pour in the milk and continue cooking, turning the rolls occasionally, until the milk begins to thicken, about 3 minutes. Stir in the butter, Parmigiano Reggiano, cream, and a pinch of salt until incorporated and the sauce has reached your desired thickness, 3 to 5 minutes.

4. Remove the toothpicks and garnish with parsley to serve.

All-purpose flour, for dredging

1½ pounds / 600 g chicken breast, thinly sliced into 6 pieces

5 ounces / 150 g prosciutto (6 slices)

2 ounces / 60 g low-moisture mozzarella cheese, shredded

Fine sea salt and freshly ground black pepper

¼ cup / 60 ml extra-virgin olive oil

½ cup / 120 ml whole milk

2 tablespoons / 30 g salted butter

5 tablespoons / 30 g grated Parmigiano Reggiano cheese

½ cup / 120 ml heavy cream

A few sprigs of fresh parsley, finely chopped

SERVES 4 TO 6

Mamma's Sunday Roast Chicken
with Marsala Gravy
page 62

MAMMA'S SUNDAY ROAST CHICKEN *with* MARSALA GRAVY

Roast Chicken

One 3- to 4-pound / 1.4 to 1.8 kg whole chicken

4 tablespoons / 60 g unsalted butter, softened

Coarse sea salt

2 large garlic cloves

1 bouquet garni (see Note)

3 medium yellow onions, halved, peel on

Extra-virgin olive oil

1 pound / 500 g (about 10) small new potatoes, quartered

Gravy

2 tablespoons / 30 g unsalted butter

1 small yellow onion, finely chopped

2 garlic cloves, minced

2 tablespoons all-purpose flour

1 cup / 250 ml dry Marsala wine or sherry

1 cup / 250 ml pan juices (if not enough, add chicken stock)

Fine sea salt and freshly ground black pepper

SERVES 4

NOTE

To make a bouquet garni, combine 5 sprigs of thyme; 1 sprig each of sage, rosemary, oregano, and parsley; and 1 bay leaf in a small bunch and tie together with kitchen twine.

After all the years of cooking countless recipes, I'm not sure whether I have signature dishes. If anything, a truly good roast chicken comes to mind, as it's an absolute staple of our household, a typical Sunday family dish that nobody cooks but me.

I've experimented with roast chicken so much, trying the many different breeds of chicken that are available here, various herbs, lemon, white wine, Jura wine, heavy on garlic or not, butter or mostly oil. Right now, I'm in love with this Italianized version with a wonderful Marsala gravy. I like to use a good Marsala; some commercial Marsala is too sweet, and while it works fine, I prefer using a better wine because it deepens the flavor and elevates the dish.

1. **Prepare the chicken.** Preheat the oven to 350°F / 180°C. Rub the outside and inside of the chicken with the butter and salt. Stuff the chicken cavity with the garlic, bouquet garni, and 1 onion half.

2. Coat the bottom of a large roasting pan or Dutch oven with a generous drizzle of olive oil. Add the potatoes and the remaining onion halves to the pan in an even layer and sprinkle with salt. Place the chicken, breastbone up, on top.

3. Roast for about 1 hour, then baste the chicken with the pan juices. Return to the oven and roast until the chicken is cooked through, about 20 minutes more. If you have a meat thermometer, it should read 160°F / 70°C.

4. Transfer the chicken to a cutting board and let rest for at least 10 minutes. Transfer the potatoes and the onions to a serving dish, leaving the pan juices behind for the gravy. Pour into a measuring cup; if you don't have 1 cup, add the chicken stock.

5. **Make the gravy.** In a medium saucepan, melt the butter over medium heat. Add the onion and sauté until softened and translucent, about 5 minutes. Add the garlic and cook until fragrant, 1 to 2 minutes more. Sprinkle with the flour, stirring continuously, until golden brown, 2 to 3 minutes.

6. Slowly pour in the wine, whisking constantly, and simmer until reduced by about half, 3 to 4 minutes. Slowly pour in the pan juices and continue simmering, stirring occasionally, until thickened, 10 to 15 minutes. Season with salt and pepper to taste.

7. Carve the chicken and serve with the potatoes and gravy on the side.

Italian Cuisine

The question I answer most often—apart from queries on how it is to have eight kids—is which food, between French and Italian, I prefer. Then the person usually remembers that I'm half Chinese and adds, "Or Chinese."

I think I answer differently every time because I feel differently every time. These are three of the best-known, most loved kitchens in the world. French food is usually viewed as elevated and complicated. Chinese food is often wrongly considered as delicious fast food that's perfect for takeaway, simply because that's how people were introduced to it. And everyone loves Italian food, although they may not have been exposed to a great variety, just the highlights of the culinary canon: pizzas, some pastas, and tiramisù.

Chinese food is in my blood. Those were my first flavors and textures, and sometimes I have intense cravings for Chinese food like I have for no other food in the world. I have a very romantic relationship with French food; that was the food I dreamed of as a child because French food meant spending time with my mother's family. It symbolized happy holidays, days in Paris with my parents, and, later, an independent life on my own.

I had no particular relationship with Italian food growing up. As a child, we frequented some Italian restaurants that served up good if not always authentic versions of Italian hits. I always liked Italian food very much, everyone does, but I had a far stronger bond with French food.

About twenty years ago, after I met my husband, we started spending most of our holidays in various parts of Italy. Doing that, you realize very quickly that not everyone in the country eats carbonara all the time. And that carbonara has no cream (okay, I did know that, but you see what I mean?). We rented houses, went to local markets, cooked at home most nights. Local food traditions fascinated me, and unlike in France, they were so diverse from one region to another. Every year, I discovered new foods that you are unlikely (or at least were then) to have in any other place than just there, where it was born.

Now that the years have passed, after living here and traveling to every region numerous times (well, except Sardinia, but that will happen soon; we always travel by train or car due to the dogs), I feel quite well versed in what Italian food is. There is no mystery involved; if you take an interest in something and apply yourself, you will, eventually, become better.

Northern cuisine is different from the cooking of the South; that's probably the great divide, but that distinction only scratches the surface. Take Piemonte, where we live, as an example. It's a mountainous region at the foot of the Alps. As is the case everywhere, temperatures are going up, but this used to be a colder climate, and locals liked to eat what you could describe as refined mountain food. They had cows and chickens and seasonal vegetables but no tomatoes or lemons, which are, to most people, icons of Italian cooking. So they ate beef and fresh pasta made with eggs, cheesy sauces or meat sauces, and raviolis stuffed with meat. Piemonte has no access to the sea, so the fish they used was the preserved type, anchovies and tuna, the latter giving birth to one of the region's signature dishes, vitello tonnato. They had an abundance of hazelnuts, which they blended with chocolate since they had less of it. Thus the gianduia chocolate was created, which then evolved into Nutella, the commercial version. The lands here are great for vineyards, so we have some of the best wine in the country, the Barolos and Barbaresco. The North as a whole is a bastion of risotto, so the locals always had some of that, too, on their tables. Desserts were made from chocolate or cream, panna cotta being the best-known recipe. In other words, not a tomato in sight. Travel the short distance down to Liguria, and everything is suddenly about basil, lemons, olives, and seafood, of course. The red sauces and the dried pastas all come from the South, and so do the pizzas. Typically they had less meat, so instead of having a steak like they do in Tuscany, they'd use it cleverly, to infuse sauces, or in meatballs, where the ingredients were stretched by adding stale bread, cheese, and herbs.

It's a well-known fact that Italians are crazy about food. What I have realized is that this quest for excellence in food, and that pride in local recipes and traditions, has a broader effect on the country as a whole. When we talk about food culture, I think we generally mean what and how people eat in a certain place. Food culture also has a big impact on Culture, with a big C. Italian food is some of the best in the world, and how much Italians care about their food elevates not only the food but society as a whole.

MARITOZZI

Sweet Buns Filled with Whipped Cream

When it comes to food cravings, I am maybe more on the savory side, but there are a few little numbers in the dessert department that will get my pulse racing. I could be walking down a street after an enormous lunch, so big that I would pledge not to have dinner, and suddenly spot, from the corner of my eye, a tray in a window, filled with the most inviting maritozzi, put there, it would seem, to devilishly tempt me. And it works every time. If I don't succumb that very minute, you can be sure I'll be back a few hours later; the thought haunting me until the maritozzi is safely in my hands. Roman maritozzis are so simple, just a fresh bun filled with whipped cream. They're genius. And as you can tell, I have an absolute weakness for whipped cream. The texture, the flavor, and maybe most of all, the idea of it. Whipped cream, to me, is like something out of a fairy tale. When people use the word *irresistible*, this is what they mean.

Buns

2 cups plus 2 tablespoons / 280 g tipo "00" or all-purpose flour

¼ cup / 50 g granulated sugar

1 teaspoon instant yeast

⅔ cup / 150 ml warm whole milk

1 large egg yolk

Grated zest of 1 lemon

1 tablespoon honey

4 tablespoons / 60 g unsalted butter, softened

¼ teaspoon fine sea salt

Vegetable oil, for greasing

1 large egg

2 tablespoons whole milk

Whipped Cream

2 cups / 500 ml heavy cream

Seeds from 1 vanilla bean

2 tablespoons powdered sugar

MAKES 12 BUNS

1. **Make the buns.** In the bowl of a stand mixer fitted with the dough hook, whisk together the flour, granulated sugar, and yeast. Create a well in the center of the mixture. Add the warm milk and egg yolk to the well. Mix on medium speed until the liquid is absorbed, about 2 minutes. Add the lemon zest and honey and continue mixing until well combined. Gradually mix in the butter until well incorporated. Add the salt and mix until the dough is elastic, 8 to 10 minutes.

2. Transfer the dough to a large greased bowl. Cover with plastic wrap and let rise in a warm place until tripled in size, about 2 hours. Line a baking sheet with parchment paper.

3. Divide the dough into 12 equal balls and place the dough balls on the prepared baking sheet. Cover with greased plastic wrap and let rise at room temperature, about 1 hour, and doubled in size.

4. Preheat the oven to 350°F / 180°C.

5. In a small bowl, beat the egg with the milk. Brush the dough balls with the egg wash. Bake until golden brown, 15 to 18 minutes. Let cool completely before filling.

6. **Make the whipped cream.** In a large bowl, use a hand mixer with a whisk attachment to whip the cream and vanilla bean seeds with the powdered sugar until stiff peaks form. Transfer the whipped cream to a piping bag.

7. Slice the cooled buns crosswise most of the way through and fill with the whipped cream.

LEMON ICE CREAM *with* VODKA

This dish is inspired by one I had in a restaurant in Venice, Da Ivo. The waiters dress in black, and they look, frankly, quite mysterious. Seeing the headwaiter prepare sorbet with vodka was a revelation. He looked so serious, like a magician onstage about to perform a magic trick, which in a way it is. I replicated the sorbet and turned it into a creamier version at home. The kids obviously have it without vodka, and we lucky parents and guests get to have the naughtier version. It's just like dinner and a show. But at home!

2½ cups / 250 g powdered sugar
⅓ cup / 80 ml lemon juice
Grated zest of 3 lemons
1¼ cups / 300 ml heavy cream

MAKES ABOUT 3 CUPS / 720 ML

1. In a medium bowl, combine the powdered sugar, lemon juice, and lemon zest until smooth.

2. In a large bowl, use a hand mixer with a whisk attachment to whip the cream until stiff peaks form. Add the lemon mixture and continue whipping until thick and fluffy.

3. Transfer to an airtight container and freeze for 6 to 8 hours.

NOTE

To add vodka for guests

Begin by scooping 1 to 2 large scoops of your homemade lemon ice cream into each guest's glass or bowl. I personally love using cocktail glasses. Use a large, elegant spoon for a professional look. Make sure the ice cream is smooth and creamy, freshly scooped from the freezer.

Pour about 1 tablespoon of vodka directly over the ice cream in each bowl or glass. If you're serving a large group, you can premeasure the vodka into a small pitcher for easy pouring at the table.

The vodka will melt the ice cream slightly, creating a creamy, boozy sauce. The alcohol adds an extra layer of flavor without overpowering the lemon.

FIOCCHI DI NEVE

Snowflakes

Size is the key here. As in bite-size. We don't always have desserts at home; a plate of seasonal fruit can be all you need, or just a coffee if it's not too late in the evening. But sometimes, after a rich main course, you just want that tiny bit of sweet on your tongue, a change of tones for your palate, even though you are too full to have anything substantial. In restaurants, we solve this problem by ordering one or two sweets for the table to share. At home, these delightful Neapolitan "snowflakes," as they are called, do the trick. They are soft and small brioche-like pastries with the lightest heavenly ricotta cream filling. What's even better is to make a big batch so you can have some for breakfast the following day as well.

Fiocchi di Neve

2 cups / 250 g manitoba flour (or bread flour) (see Note)

1½ teaspoons active dry yeast

⅓ cup / 65 g granulated sugar

1 large egg

Pinch of fine sea salt

½ cup / 125 ml whole milk

4 tablespoons / 60 g unsalted butter, at room temperature

Filling

⅔ cup / 150 ml whole milk

Seeds from ¼ vanilla bean, or ½ teaspoon vanilla extract

2 tablespoons cornstarch

4 ounces / 170 g ricotta cheese

⅓ cup / 65 g superfine sugar

1 tablespoon honey

¾ cup / 180 ml heavy cream

2 tablespoons powdered sugar, plus more for dusting

MAKES 26 FIOCCHI DI NEVE

1. **Make the fiocchi di neve.** In the bowl of a stand mixer fitted with the dough hook, combine the flour, yeast, granulated sugar, egg, and salt. Add half of the milk, 4 tablespoons / 60 ml, and mix on medium-low speed until well combined. Increase the speed to medium and mix until the dough is elastic, 10 minutes. Gradually add the remaining milk and then slowly incorporate the butter in two batches, waiting for the dough to absorb each dose before adding the next.

2. Transfer the dough to a large greased bowl and let rise, covered with a damp cloth, in a warm place until doubled in size, about 2 hours.

3. Divide the dough into 26 balls. Place the dough balls on a baking sheet and let rise, covered with a damp cloth, until doubled in size, about 1 hour.

4. Preheat the oven to 375°F/190°C.

5. Bake until golden brown, 10 to 12 minutes. Let cool completely.

6. **Make the filling.** In a small saucepan, combine the milk and vanilla over medium-low heat. Add the cornstarch and whisk gently until the mixture thickens, 5 to 10 minutes. Let cool for 30 minutes.

7. In a small bowl, combine the ricotta, superfine sugar, and honey. In a medium bowl, using a hand mixer with a whisk attachment, whip the cream and powdered sugar until stiff peaks form. Fold the ricotta mixture into the whipped cream mixture, then fold in the milk custard gently. Slip a narrow pastry tip (like an Ateco Bismark tip) into a piping bag and then transfer the filling to the piping bag.

8. Line a baking sheet with parchment paper. Insert the piping tip into the base of each bun and fill. Transfer the filled buns to the prepared baking sheet. Dust with powdered sugar before serving.

NOTE

In Italy, I learned about manitoba flour, as it is often used for making panettone, baba, and doughnuts. Its strength and elasticity are ideal.

ZEPPOLE *with* RICOTTA CREAM

Sometimes after finishing a meal, or even between meals, I find myself craving a little something, but I don't really know what. Chances are it's this perfect bite, with a cup of espresso.

Zeppole are simple doughnuts, powdered with sugar. They originate in Rome but have spread across the South. When I have time and I'm expecting the kids back from school in an hour or two, I like to whip up the dough—it's the kind of recipe that requires no unusual ingredients. When I hear them walk through the front door, I'm ready to drop in the first batch, a beautiful moment for me and for them, and of course I have one or two zeppole myself. I added the ricotta cream filling version just in case you wanted something more decadent, but they are delicious with or without!

Zeppole

1 cup / 250 ml whole milk

8 tablespoons / 115 g unsalted butter

2 tablespoons granulated sugar

¼ teaspoon fine sea salt

1 cup / 120 g tipo "00" or all-purpose flour

4 large eggs

Vegetable oil, for frying

Powdered sugar, for dusting

Filling (optional)

1¼ cups / 300 g ricotta cheese

2 tablespoons superfine sugar

Grated zest of ½ lemon

1 cup / 250 ml heavy cream

½ teaspoon vanilla extract

MAKES 8 ZEPPOLE

1. Cut out eight 5-inch / 12 cm squares of parchment paper. Trace 3½-inch / 9 cm circles on the backs of each square.

2. **Make the zeppole.** In a medium saucepan, bring the milk, butter, granulated sugar, and salt to a boil, stirring gently, over low heat. Remove the pan from the heat. Add the flour and mix vigorously with a wooden spoon until the dough pulls away from the edges of the pan and forms a smooth ball.

3. Return the pan to medium heat, stirring, until the dough dries out slightly, 3 to 4 minutes. Transfer the dough to the bowl of a stand mixer fitted with the paddle attachment.

4. Mix the dough on medium-low speed until cooled, about 5 minutes. Add the eggs, one at a time, mixing after each addition until incorporated into the dough. Transfer the dough to a pastry bag fitted with a ½-inch / 1 cm star tip.

5. Line a baking sheet with paper towels. Pour 2 inches / 5 cm oil into a large, high-sided pan. Heat the oil to about 350°F / 180°C over medium heat. You can test whether the oil is hot enough by dropping in a small piece of dough. If the dough turns golden within seconds, the oil is ready.

6. Pipe a thin layer of dough inside each circle on the parchment paper. Pipe a border around each circle to create a nest shape.

7. Working in batches, add the zeppole to the oil, parchment side up. Fry for about 1 minute, then carefully remove the parchment paper with tongs. Turn the zeppole over and fry, turning frequently, until golden, about another 5 minutes. Transfer to the prepared baking sheet and let cool.

8. **Make the filling (optional).** In the bowl of a stand mixer fitted with the whisk attachment, mix the ricotta and sugar on medium-high speed until smooth, 2 to 3 minutes. Add the zest, cream, and vanilla and mix on high speed until stiff peaks form. Transfer to a clean pastry bag fitted with a fluted tip.

9. Fill the cavities of each zeppola with ricotta cream, if using, and dust with powdered sugar.

MY BIRTHDAY CAKE

I'm not sure there is such a thing as the perfect birthday cake, or maybe they are all perfect in their own way. What I do know is that I love the candle-blowing moment. So much so that we do it several times throughout the special day. It starts in the morning, typically with waffles or pancakes, even on top of toast. Then it continues with the dessert after lunch and the dessert after dinner. If both meals are enjoyed out at restaurants, I still insist on making a birthday cake at home for teatime. With candles every time, of course.

My husband thinks I'm over the top; he's a minimalist and believes you should have one cake, once. I simply have to disagree. You can never have too many birthday cakes, especially when they are as good as this one. We used to experiment with different cakes, but this is my current favorite: rich in chocolate, covered simply in whipped cream, and decorated with whichever fruits are in season.

Cake

2 cups / 240 g tipo "00" or all-purpose flour

1 cup / 200 g superfine sugar

½ cup / 50 g unsweetened cocoa powder

1½ teaspoons baking powder

1½ teaspoons baking soda

½ teaspoon fine sea salt

1 cup / 250 ml buttermilk

2 large eggs

8 tablespoons / 115 g unsalted butter, melted, plus more for greasing the pans

1 tablespoon vanilla extract

1 cup / 250 ml boiling water

1 cup / 150 g fresh raspberries (or halved strawberries)

Topping

1 cup / 250 ml heavy cream

8 ounces / 225 g mascarpone cheese

½ cup / 60 g powdered sugar

SERVES 6

1. Preheat the oven to 350°F / 180°C. Grease two 8-inch / 20 cm cake pans with butter and line the bottoms with a round of parchment paper.

2. **Make the cake.** In a medium bowl, sift together the flour, superfine sugar, cocoa powder, baking powder, baking soda, and salt.

3. In a large bowl, whisk together the buttermilk, eggs, melted butter, and vanilla. Add the dry ingredients and whisk until well combined. Add the boiling water and whisk until well combined and the batter is runny.

4. Divide the batter between the prepared cake pans and bake until a toothpick inserted into the center comes out clean, about 30 minutes. Let cool in the pans on a wire rack for 5 minutes, then remove from the pans and set aside to cool completely.

5. **Once the cakes are cool, make the topping.** In a large bowl, using a hand mixer with a whisk attachment, whip the cream, mascarpone, and powdered sugar until stiff peaks form.

6. Spread half of the cream over one of the cakes and scatter with half the berries. Top with the second cake and spread with the remaining cream and berries.

Estate / Summer

TORTA DI CRESPELLE E POMODORI

Layered Pancake with Tomatoes

If you are holding this book and considering which recipe to cook, I would pick this one. Not just because it's one of my absolute favorites, but because I think it will be one of yours, too. We first had this recipe at a friend's castle in Umbria. Our friend, a marchese no less, is a kind man with simple but good taste in food. He always asks his resident cook, Monica, to make this for him when he stays at the castle with his wife. In fact, he asks for torta di crespelle every night until his wife suggests something else, for the sake of variety. When I had the cake for the first time, I didn't pay enough attention to how it was made, but I fell in love at first bite. So I asked Monica to make it again (much to the pleasure of the marchese), and this time I videotaped the process, just to make sure I got all the steps right.

I love making this dish at home; it's simple but quite unusual and not something you can find in restaurants—you have to be lucky enough to be invited to someone's house.

Grazie, Giovanni and Tara, for having us.

Pancake Batter

6 large eggs

1 cup / 120 g all-purpose flour

1¾ cups / 400 ml whole milk

Fine sea salt and freshly ground black pepper

20 cherry tomatoes, thinly sliced

2 tablespoons extra-virgin olive oil

Mayonnaise

4 large egg yolks

½ teaspoon fine sea salt

½ teaspoon freshly ground black pepper, plus a pinch for garnish

¼ cup / 60 ml extra-virgin olive oil

1. **Make the pancake batter.** In a large bowl, whisk together the eggs, flour, milk, and a pinch of salt until smooth. Let the batter rest for 10 to 15 minutes.

2. Heat a medium nonstick skillet over medium heat. Add a small ladle of batter (enough to fill the pan) and swirl to spread evenly. Cook until golden brown, 1 to 2 minutes per side. Repeat with the remaining batter, stacking the pancakes on a plate as you go.

3. In a large bowl, toss the tomatoes with the olive oil. Season with salt and pepper to taste.

4. **Make the mayonnaise.** In a medium bowl, whisk together the egg yolks and salt and pepper. Gradually add the olive oil, whisking constantly, until the mixture thickens and emulsifies. Adjust the seasoning to taste.

5. Place one pancake on a serving plate. Spread with a thin layer of the mayonnaise, then evenly top with a layer of the tomatoes. Repeat with the remaining pancakes, mayonnaise, and tomatoes, ending with a pancake on top.

6. Cover the cake with plastic wrap and refrigerate for at least 1 hour.

7. Before serving, garnish the top pancake with any remaining tomatoes and a pinch of pepper. Slice into wedges and serve chilled.

PIZZA DI SCAROLA

Escarole-Stuffed Pizza

I used to serve escarole mostly raw as a salad or perhaps sautéed as a side dish, like spinach or Swiss chard. This "pizza," which is found everywhere in Campania, changed my mind. Not to be confused with a pizza napoletana, this is more of a shortcrust-like pastry with a savory stuffing. Pastry shops, food stands, and gastronomias (delis) make pizza di scarola before noon, and locals pass by throughout the day and grab a slice. It's the perfect picnic food, accompanied with mozzarella and tomatoes, salads, and such, but a small slice also works very well as a starter.

The raisins add a bit of tart-sweetness, which I think is a great touch.

Dough

3½ teaspoons active dry yeast

1 cup / 250 ml lukewarm water

4 cups / 500 g tipo "00" or all-purpose flour

1 teaspoon fine sea salt

Juice of 1 lemon

Filling

7 tablespoons / 100 ml extra-virgin olive oil

1 garlic clove, slightly crushed

5 to 6 oil-packed anchovy fillets

3 heads escarole, coarsely chopped

3 tablespoons raisins, soaked and drained

1½ ounces / 40 g black olives, pitted

3 tablespoons pine nuts

Fine sea salt and freshly ground black pepper

Assembly

1 tablespoon olive oil, to grease the pie plate

1 large egg yolk

2 tablespoons whole milk

SERVES 6

1. **Make the dough.** In a large bowl, combine the yeast with 3½ tablespoons / 50 ml of the lukewarm water. Once the yeast is dissolved, add the flour, salt, lemon juice, and remaining water. Knead the ingredients together by hand until you have a smooth mass, 8 to 10 minutes. Cover the dough and let rise at room temperature until doubled in size, about 2 hours.

2. **Make the filling.** In a large sauté pan, heat 2 tablespoons of the olive oil over medium heat. Add the garlic and stir until golden, 5 minutes. Discard the garlic. Add the anchovies to the pan and let them dissolve in the oil, breaking them up gently with a wooden spoon. Add the escarole, raisins, olives, and pine nuts. Add the remaining olive oil and toss gently while cooking. Season with salt and pepper and cook, stirring, until softened and cooked through, about 5 minutes. Drain any excess water from the pan and let the filling cool.

3. Divide the dough into 2 balls. Place the dough balls on a floured work surface. Working with one at a time and starting from the center and working toward the edge, press firmly with your palm to flatten into an 8-inch / 20 cm round. Lift the dough and rotate until you get a 10-inch / 25 cm round.

4. Preheat the oven to 350°F / 180°C. Grease a 9-inch / 23 cm pie plate with the olive oil.

5. **Assemble the pizza.** Press one dough round into the bottom and sides of the prepared pie plate. Prick the dough with a fork. Add the filling, then top with the other dough round, pinching the edges to seal. Cut a vent in the center of the dough.

6. In a small bowl, beat the egg yolk with the milk. Brush the dough with the egg wash. Bake until golden, about 45 minutes. Let cool, then slice and serve.

STUFFED PEPPERS *with* YESTERDAY'S SPAGHETTI

Another contender for my favorite of the book and a dish you cannot always easily find in restaurants, at least not good versions. Italian cuisine is much more diverse and varied than people think. If you're in a restaurant in, say, Naples, and they offer national classics like Milanese, carbonara, and panna cotta, you are probably in the wrong place. If, however, they have hard-to-find regional plates that feel like home cooking, you've most likely hit the jackpot.

Over the years we've had this dish a few times, but the best version, in my opinion, is the one they make at Ristorante Europeo Mattozzi (like the spring soup on page 33). It's an ingenious way of serving spaghetti, especially leftovers. I have a big weakness for all things stuffed, baked, and layered, and here we tick all those boxes.

6 tablespoons / 90 ml extra-virgin olive oil, plus more for drizzling

2 garlic cloves, crushed

2 cups / 200 g cooked spaghetti (leftover from the previous day is perfect)

1 teaspoon fresh oregano, chopped finely

Fine sea salt and freshly ground black pepper

1¼ cups / 150 g diced fresh mozzarella cheese

½ cup / 50 g grated Parmigiano Reggiano cheese

4 large long peppers, tops cut off (and reserved) and deseeded

Fresh basil leaves, chopped, for garnish

SERVES 4

1. Preheat the oven to 350°F / 180°C.

2. In a large skillet, heat the olive oil over medium heat. Add the garlic and cook, stirring, until fragrant, 2 minutes. Discard the garlic. Add the cooked spaghetti and oregano to the pan and season with salt and pepper to taste. Add the mozzarella and ¼ cup / 25 g of the Parmigiano Reggiano and cook, stirring, until the cheese is melted and combined.

3. Gently stuff each pepper with the spaghetti mixture. Arrange the stuffed peppers with their tops in a baking dish.

4. Sprinkle the stuffed pepper with the remaining ¼ cup / 25 g Parmigiano Reggiano and drizzle with olive oil. Bake until the cheese is golden, about 30 minutes. To serve, garnish with basil and more olive oil, if desired.

FRITTATA DI SPAGHETTI

I'm a true believer in what is often called cucina povera (peasant food), the idea that when you have limited access to expensive ingredients, you make the most of them when you have them, and when you don't, you get creative. This pasta cake is probably the best version of using leftover pasta I have ever seen, and the most beautiful, too. There is something so satisfying about bringing back to life an unappetizing bowl of cold spaghetti, by mixing in eggs and whatever hams or sausages and cheese you have in the fridge. The result is such a beauty, and it gives me intense pleasure to serve it, especially to guests. This is alchemy in cooking.

As this is technically a pasta dish, it could be considered a primi, and maybe it is, but I prefer to think of it as a starter or a snack—picnic food, as I keep calling it.

1½ cups / 350 g cooked spaghetti

2 tablespoons extra-virgin olive oil, plus more for drizzling

6 large eggs

1½ cups / 150 g grated Parmigiano Reggiano cheese

1 teaspoon fine sea salt

1 teaspoon freshly ground black pepper

3½ ounces / 100 g provolone or mozzarella cheese, sliced

5 ounces / 150 g chopped Italian sausage or sliced mortadella

A handful of fresh basil, chopped

SERVES 6

1. Place the spaghetti in a large bowl, drizzle with the olive oil, and toss well to evenly combine. In a medium bowl, beat the eggs with the Parmigiano Reggiano and season with the salt and pepper. Add the egg mixture to the bowl with the pasta and toss gently.

2. In a 10-inch / 25 cm skillet, heat the 2 tablespoons olive oil over medium-high heat. Add half the pasta mixture in an even layer. Top with the provolone and sausage and sprinkle with the basil. Top with the remaining spaghetti mixture. Cover and cook until the bottom is golden, about 8 minutes, turning the pan gradually clockwise to cook evenly. Lift the base of the spaghetti frittata to check if it's evenly golden brown and firm. Then flip and cook, covered, until golden, 8 minutes more.

3. Transfer to a serving plate and let cool slightly before slicing and serving.

Our Italian Kitchen

We moved to Turin over six years ago, and it's been a beautiful experience. We were so nostalgic about the country house we left behind that we brought almost nothing with us. We left our French home entirely intact, maybe so we could return one day and find everything how we remembered. And for a while we did, for holidays and small escapes. My French kitchen was glorious: a beautiful, large room with white-and-red tiled flooring and a stove big enough to cook for forty people. Easily. Next to the kitchen we had a pantry and prep room filled with old furniture from a retired butcher. Then two dining rooms, one with a table so large it could seat thirty people. We called that room the Harvest Room, named after the grape pickers who had dined there in times gone by. Finally, at the front of the house, we had another, smaller kitchen that was colder and served as an entry point for fresh produce. That's where the mushrooms got cleaned, the stock was made, the fish gutted, the chickens deboned. We called the small kitchen the Boucherie because of the large and heavy butcher's table (it took seven men and a huge effort to install it). The Boucherie was always full of the freshest produce, vegetables and fruits from the markets and our own kitchen garden; flowers that hadn't yet been put in vases; cheeses; and cases of wine. For a cook, that house was a dream.

Which brings us to Turin.

We chose our current apartment because it was grand and beautiful and considerably larger than our previous one. All the children have more space to grow and create, the street in front of our building is lined with sycamore trees, so the view from our windows in summer is a most delightful panoply of fluffy green. Mostly we chose it because unlike so many apartments where everything or at least some rooms have been renovated or restored, everything was original. The gorgeous hardwood floors needed some love, which we gave. The master bathroom was untouched, and we left it that way (the bathtub could be larger, but we wouldn't dream of updating it). Don't get me started on the ceilings. Our kitchen has old floors and old tiles, some cracked, but that's fine. It opens up onto a small balcony, covered by a rusty metal greenhouse-like structure. The first time I stepped into that kitchen it was almost empty, just a free-standing old stove and a table in a corner with a small sink. The covered balcony creates a wonderful dimension from that angle and lets in muted light. I immediately named the balcony the Limonaia, like the rooms or structures used to shelter citrus trees in winter here in Italy. I pictured myself at an imaginary stove, popping out to the Limonaia to cut some herbs for my cooking. "I think this is the place," I said to Oddur. He agreed.

It isn't as big as our country kitchen in France. We're in town, after all, but for an old Italian city kitchen, it's very large. It feels in many ways like a reincarnation, similar hues and textures, same rustic feel. A kitchen where you can open oysters and don't have to worry about the liquor staining the floor. Where you can scale fish and clean artichokes and spill some oil or wine without drama. A kitchen that can stand up to any cooking—that was the first requirement.

(It sounds obvious, but in my experience it's not. I see photographs of often very beautiful kitchens in magazines and my first thought is "Dear lord, how is anyone ever going to cook in that thing?")

My second requirement was to have a dining table inside the kitchen, where we could all have meals together. This meant sacrificing a "cooking island," which would have provided more workspace and storage. I had a table in mind—it was already ours—waiting for us in our house in France. While it's a little low, it doubles as a work counter and is very used to our family; we give it love and abuse in equal measure. In addition to the dining table, we have a large enough stove (although I compromised on what exactly is a large enough stove; it was that or no dishwasher), marble worktops, a very big fridge and freezer, and ample storage.

We wanted a kitchen that looked like it had always been there, and I think we succeeded. A kitchen you walk into and you don't particularly study the design but where you see the people and notice the food. For that is what a kitchen is to me: a stage for ingredients to shine and to be appreciated by the audience, the people who are lucky enough to eat them.

My husband was happy to accept my takeover of the small corridor to the dining room as more kitchen storage. Likely because he saw that as a fine home for the machines he deems most useful: the espresso maker, the coffee grinder, and the meat slicer. As I write this, we have spread farther down the corridor and claimed cabinets for provisions, canned tomatoes, mustards, pickles, and condiments. At this rate, the kitchen will eat the apartment whole.

It wasn't all easy. We had to break up the floor and part of the wall to move the sink, then lovingly put it back. An August hailstorm shattered many of the old windows in the Limonaia, so we had to replace them with similar ones. The electricity was an issue for a while and so was the plumbing. The only thing that was easy were the bespoke Tuscan cabinets that went in as fast and as smoothly as whipped cream on a Sunday.

One night, when it was all coming together, when nothing was ready but the kitchen (almost) and the rest of the apartment was covered in dust and plastic, I sat down at the kitchen table, poured myself a glass of wine, and just felt the room. That's when I knew I was home.

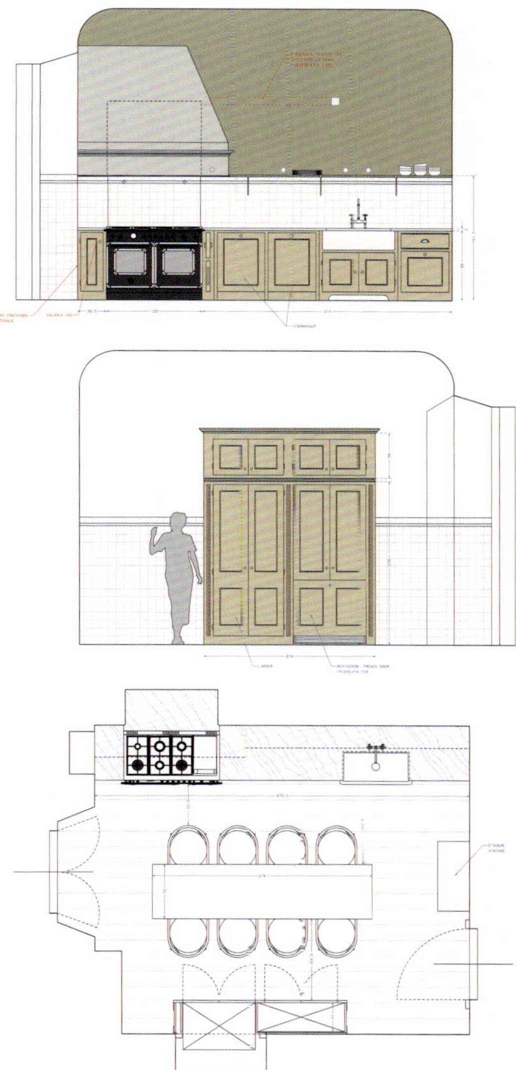

Courtesy of Paolo Badesco & Partners

SUMMER HOLIDAY CREAMY LEMON PASTA

For our family, lemons are often, maybe always, associated with soaring temperatures. In the Bay of Naples, where we like to spend our summer holiday, we always buy a full crate of lemons. Nothing makes a kitchen by the sea look more beautiful than stacks of lemon. We stuff them in roast chicken, squeeze them over salads and grilled fish, slice them for our summer cocktails. Usually we can't keep up, and when the already mature lemons (spring is really their prime) are starting to show their age, I make this delicious pasta that to us sings of summer. Then we buy another crate of lemons and start again. Serve it with chilled Italian white wine (preferably from Naples, like a Greco di Tufo), with a few slices of yellow peaches added, just as they do at one of my favorite restaurants in Napoli.

1 pound / 500 g dried spaghetti

2 tablespoons extra-virgin olive oil

2 tablespoons / 30 g unsalted butter

Grated zest of 2 lemons

1 garlic clove, thinly sliced

Juice of 3 lemons

Fine sea salt and freshly ground black pepper

¾ cup / 180 ml heavy cream

1 cup / 100 g freshly grated Parmigiano Reggiano cheese, plus more for garnish

A few sprigs of fresh parsley, finely chopped

A few sprigs of fresh mint, leaves finely chopped

SERVES 4 TO 6

1. Bring a large pot of salted water to a boil over high heat. Add the pasta and cook to al dente according to the package directions. Reserving a ladleful of pasta water, drain the pasta.

2. In a large sauté pan, heat the olive oil and butter over medium heat. Add the lemon zest and garlic and cook, stirring, until it sizzles, then stir in the lemon juice. Cook until slightly reduced, 3 minutes, then season with salt and pepper to taste. Add the cream and the reserved ladle of pasta water and stir to combine. Add the pasta, sprinkle the Parmigiano Reggiano evenly over the top, and stir gently.

3. Serve with a sprinkle of Parmigiano Reggiano, parsley, and mint.

LASAGNA *with* PESTO, GREEN BEANS & POTATOES

Another layered pasta dish that I am crazy about. Many of the dishes in this section can trace their origins to the South of Italy, but here we are most definitely in the North. These are Ligurian flavors at their best. If you want to deconstruct this dish, I guess you could just say it is Ligurian pesto served as a lasagna, with the added comfort of green beans and potatoes in each bite.

I like to let the lasagna strips stick out a bit so the ends turn a little crispy and golden in the oven. At home, I prepare this lasagna in a big dish that holds enough for the whole family, but when I serve it at dinner parties, I enjoy making individual portions in baking dishes for each guest, which is more elegant and makes the serving easier.

Pesto

4 cups / 120 g fresh basil leaves, plus more for garnish

½ cup / 65 g pine nuts

1 cup / 100 g grated Parmigiano Reggiano cheese

3 garlic cloves

1 cup / 250 ml extra-virgin olive oil, plus more for greasing the pan

Fine sea salt and freshly ground black pepper

Béchamel

4 tablespoons / 60 g unsalted butter

½ cup / 60 g all-purpose flour

4 cups / 1 liter whole milk

Pinch of ground nutmeg

Fine sea salt and freshly ground black pepper

Assembly

10 ounces / 300 g new potatoes

7 ounces / 200 g green beans (haricots verts)

8 ounces / 250 g fresh lasagna sheets

2 cups / 200 g grated Parmigiano Reggiano cheese

SERVES 4

1. **Make the pesto.** In a food processor, combine the basil, pine nuts, Parmigiano Reggiano, and garlic and pulse for about 2 minutes, until finely chopped and well combined. With the processor running, slowly add the olive oil in a single stream and pulse until the mixture is smooth but not runny. Season with salt and pepper to taste.

2. **Make the béchamel.** In a medium saucepan, melt the butter over medium heat. Add the flour and whisk continuously until the mixture is smooth and bubbling, about 2 minutes. Gradually begin adding the milk, whisking constantly to prevent lumps, until the sauce is thick enough to coat the back of a spoon. Season with nutmeg, salt, and pepper to taste.

3. **Cook the vegetables.** Rinse the potatoes. Trim the green beans and cut them into 2-inch / 5 cm pieces.

4. Place the potatoes in a large pot of salted water. Bring to a boil over medium-high heat, reduce the heat to medium, and cook until soft when poked with a fork, 10 to 15 minutes.

5. Add the green beans to the pot with the potatoes. Let everything cook together until the beans are tender but still a little crisp, another 4 to 6 minutes. Drain the vegetables and let cool for 10 minutes. Once the potatoes are cool enough to handle, peel them and slice them into thin rounds.

6. **Assemble the lasagna.** Preheat the oven to 350°F / 180°C. Grease a 9 × 13-inch / 23 × 33 cm baking dish with olive oil.

7. Spread a thin layer of béchamel on the bottom of the prepared baking dish. Top with a layer of lasagna sheets. Spread a thin layer of béchamel over the lasagna, then dollop with the pesto and sprinkle with some of the Parmigiano Reggiano. Scatter with a third of the potatoes and green beans. Repeat twice, ending with three layers with the last of the lasagna, béchamel, and cheese.

8. Bake until the top is golden and bubbly, 30 minutes. Let cool for 10 minutes. Garnish with basil before serving.

FRESCA

Gnocchi alla Sorrentina
page 102

GNOCCHI ALLA SORRENTINA

Sorrento is a beautiful town overlooking the Bay of Naples. Like many seaside towns in Italy, it is distinctly old-fashioned, with a touch of retro glamour and a '60s vibe. Sorrento is perched on a cliff, which makes the views all the more impressive. Like most of the region, it's frequented by tourists, although not as overwhelmingly so as Capri or Positano. In popular culture, Sorrento is famous for two things: the song "Come Back to Sorrento" ("Torna a Surriento"), made famous by the likes of Pavarotti, and this heavenly dish, Gnocchi alla Sorrentina.

I rarely make it during our summer holidays as it's readily available in local restaurants, and the young children love it so much I think it accounts for almost half of their food intake when we're out. So while this is a summer pasta, I most often cook it at home in other seasons, when we are all wishing for summer. It's also a perfect date night dish for the family, when Oddur and I have other plans for the rest of the evening. I buy fresh gnocchi from a local pastificio, quickly make the sauce, and slide it in the oven before kissing them good night.

Gnocchi (makes 60 to 70 gnocchi, or use 1 pound / 500 g store-bought gnocchi)

14 ounces / 400 g yellow potatoes

2 large egg yolks

1 teaspoon fine sea salt

1 cup / 120 g all-purpose flour

Pinch of ground nutmeg

Sauce

2 tablespoons extra-virgin olive oil

1 garlic clove

6 ounces / 170 g datterini or cherry tomatoes, blanched (see Note), peeled, and halved

Fine sea salt

Assembly

7 ounces / 200 g fresh mozzarella cheese, cubed

A handful of fresh basil leaves, coarsely chopped, for garnish

½ cup / 45 g shaved Parmigiano Reggiano cheese (optional)

SERVES 4

1. **Make the gnocchi.** Place the potatoes in a large pot of salted water. Bring to a boil over medium-high heat and cook until very tender, about 40 minutes. Remove the potatoes with a slotted spoon and drain. Reserve the pot of water for cooking the gnocchi later.

2. Let the potatoes cool for 5 minutes, then peel. Place them in a ricer and rice the potatoes into a large bowl. Make a small well in the center of the potatoes. Add the egg yolks and salt and beat the eggs with a fork until smooth. Add the flour and nutmeg and mix slowly with a wooden spoon until you get a stiff dough.

3. Transfer the mixture to a floured work surface. Use your dough scraper to gather everything neatly. Gently knead the dough until smooth but slightly sticky, about 3 minutes.

4. When the dough is smooth and homogeneous, form it into cylindrical dough strips. Cut them into small pieces, about ¾ inch / 2 cm, like little pillows, to make the gnocchi.

5. **Make the sauce.** In a medium skillet (ovenproof if you have it), heat the olive oil over medium heat. Add the garlic and cook until golden, 3 minutes. Remove the garlic and reduce the heat to low. Add the tomatoes and season with salt. Cook, stirring, until softened, about 5 minutes.

6. Return the reserved pot of water to a boil. Add the gnocchi and cook until they rise to the surface, about 1 minute. Drain immediately.

7. Preheat the broiler. Add the gnocchi to the skillet with the tomatoes and stir gently. If your skillet is not ovenproof, transfer the mixture to a 12-inch / 30 cm round baking dish. Top the gnocchi with the mozzarella and place 5 inches / 13 cm under the broiler until golden and bubbly, 4 to 6 minutes (watch carefully).

8. Garnish with basil and shaved Parmigiano Reggiano (if using).

NOTE

To blanch the tomatoes, add them to a pot of boiling water for about 10 seconds, then immediately transfer them to a bowl of ice water.

SPAGHETTI ALLA NERANO

Every dish comes from somewhere, and while most Italian dishes are attributed to a region or a fairly large city, this one bears the name of a tiny beach town not far from Sorrento (which is known for its gnocchi dish, page 102) and the more famous Positano. The key ingredients here are simple, as they often are in Italian cooking, and this may be one of the finest examples I can think of where the abundant zucchinis of summer are put to proper use. I wouldn't say zucchinis are maligned, but I don't think they're many people's favorite vegetable.

Here they take top billing, or at least they share it with the cheese. Simple ingredients, yes, but as with many plain pasta dishes, it's all in the preparation. It's important to create a rich emulsion from just the zucchini, oil, and cooking water before mixing in the perfectly cooked pasta and finally the cheese. The result is endlessly rewarding and certainly more than the sum of its parts.

Vegetable oil, for frying

1½ pounds / 700 g medium zucchini, sliced in ⅛-inch / 3 mm thick rounds

Fine sea salt and freshly ground black pepper

1 pound / 500 g dried spaghetti

5 tablespoons / 75 ml extra-virgin olive oil

1 garlic clove, finely sliced

2½ cups / 225 g grated cheese of your choice (I like Parmigiano Reggiano, Bebè di Sorrento, and/or caciocavallo)

A few sprigs of fresh basil, leaves chopped

SERVES 4

1. Line a plate with paper towels. Pour 2 inches / 5 cm oil into a large, high-sided pan. Heat the oil to about 375°F / 190°C over medium heat. You can test whether the oil is hot enough by dropping in a small piece of bread. If it browns quickly, the oil is ready. Working in batches, add the zucchini and fry until golden, 4 to 5 minutes. Transfer to the paper towel–lined plate. Let cool completely, making sure to drain as much oil as possible. Season with salt and pepper.

2. Bring a large pot of salted water to a boil over high heat. Add the pasta and cook for 6 minutes. Reserving 1 cup / 250 ml of the pasta water, drain the pasta.

3. In a large nonstick skillet, heat the olive oil over medium heat. Add the garlic and sauté until golden, about 2 minutes. Reduce the heat to low. Add the zucchini and cook gently until softened, about 3 minutes. Increase the heat to high and add ½ cup / 125 ml of the reserved pasta water and reduce until thickened, about 2 minutes. Add the drained spaghetti and toss everything together.

4. Remove the pan from the heat, then add the grated cheese and the remaining ½ cup / 125 ml pasta water. Toss evenly to combine. Let the pasta cool slightly, then add the basil. Season with pepper and serve.

ORECCHIETTE *with* ROASTED FRESH TOMATOES & STRACCIATELLA

This pasta dish defines summers in Italy, and the plump, ruby-red tomatoes bursting with flavor are the stars of the show here. The tomatoes are roasted to intensify their natural sweetness and pair beautifully with luxurious stracciatella cheese, the creamy heart of burrata. The combination of flavors—sweet, tangy tomatoes with the luscious cheese—is nothing short of divine. And the orecchiette is a very satisfying pasta to eat: It's almost chewy but in a good way. This recipe is more than just a meal; it's a nostalgic journey to those idyllic summer days in Puglia.

12 ounces / 350 g cherry tomatoes, halved

2 sprigs of fresh rosemary

1 garlic clove, crushed

3 tablespoons extra-virgin olive oil, plus more for drizzling and serving

Fine sea salt and freshly ground black pepper

1 pound / 500 g dried orecchiette pasta

1 garlic clove, thinly sliced

1 teaspoon crushed red pepper flakes

12 ounces / 350 g stracciatella or burrata cheese

A handful of fresh basil leaves, for garnish

SERVES 4

1. Preheat the oven to 375°F / 190°C.

2. Arrange the tomatoes, rosemary, and crushed garlic on a baking sheet and drizzle with olive oil. Sprinkle with salt and black pepper. Roast until the tomatoes are golden and charred, about 25 minutes. Discard the rosemary and garlic.

3. Bring a large pot of salted water to a boil over high heat. Add the pasta and cook to al dente according to the package directions. Reserving 1 cup / 250 ml pasta water, drain the pasta.

4. In a large sauté pan, heat the 3 tablespoons olive oil over medium heat. Add the sliced garlic and cook until golden, about 2 minutes. Increase the heat to high. Add the pepper flakes, roasted tomatoes, and half of the reserved pasta water and sauté until well combined, 2 minutes more. Season with salt to taste.

5. Add the drained pasta and the remaining reserved pasta water to the pan and mix to combine. Season with black pepper.

6. Serve immediately topped with the stracciatella, basil leaves, and a drizzle of olive oil.

Spaghetti & Meatballs *with* Pine Nuts
page 114

GRILLED FISH *with* LEMON & HERBS

It is sometimes said that if you give a French chef an ingredient, a protein like meat or fish, that they will instinctively think, "What can I do with this? How can I alter it, enhance it? How can I best impose upon this simple piece of fish my impressive cooking skills?" On the other hand, an Italian chef will study the ingredients and think what he always thinks: "Maybe olive oil and salt are enough. Some herbs, or a squeeze of lemon juice. At the most." This is an oversimplification, of course, and things have evolved in both kitchens. Still, there is, and always has been, a certain truth to the cliché.

On the island of Procida, where we spend our summers, they have the freshest fish imaginable. The fish markets open in the afternoon when the local fishing boats return, and whenever I pass by (or send my husband or kids) on the way home from the beach, we pick up what looks most appealing to us from the day's catch.

¼ cup / 60 ml extra-virgin olive oil

Grated zest and juice of 1 lemon, plus another sliced for garnish

3 small shallots, finely sliced

2 tablespoons chopped fresh parsley

1 tablespoon fresh thyme leaves

1 tablespoon chopped fresh rosemary

Fine sea salt and freshly ground black pepper

Four 5- to 6-ounce / 140 to 170 g sea bass fillets

Sprigs of fresh basil, for garnish

SERVES 4

1. In a small bowl, whisk together the olive oil, lemon zest and juice, shallots, parsley, thyme, rosemary, and salt and pepper to taste.

2. Pat the fish dry and place in a shallow dish. Pour the marinade over the fish and turn to coat. Cover and refrigerate for at least 30 minutes or up to 2 hours.

3. Preheat the grill to medium-high heat (about 375° to 400°F / 190° to 200°C).

4. Letting any excess marinade drip off, add the fish to the grill. Grill until charred, 3 to 4 minutes per side.

5. Serve garnished with lemon slices and basil.

SEA BREAM ALL'ACQUA PAZZA *with* CRISPY POTATOES

Crazy water, that's what *acqua pazza* means. So this is a traditional Neapolitan recipe for fish in crazy water, except it's not so crazy—just a simple, fresh white fish poached in tomato-infused water or broth. It can range from very brothy to a slightly thicker, saucier consistency based on what you want. Countless versions exist, but the main principles remain the same, and most versions include some herbs, olives, and garlic or onions. My family loves all things tomato, so this is an ideal way to prepare fresh fish when we've had our fill of the simpler grilled fish with lemon (page 118). I like to serve our acqua pazza with potatoes and some fresh bitter greens like arugula.

Potatoes

1 pound / 500 g russet potatoes, peeled and very thinly sliced with a mandoline

2 tablespoons extra-virgin olive oil

Fine sea salt and freshly ground black pepper

Acqua Pazza

¼ cup / 60 ml extra-virgin olive oil

3 garlic cloves, thinly sliced

1 small onion, finely chopped

1 cup / 200 g cherry tomatoes, halved

1 cup / 250 ml dry white wine

1 cup / 250 ml fish or vegetable stock

Grated zest of ½ lemon

2 tablespoons capers, rinsed

1 whole sea bream (about 3 pounds / 1.3 kg), cleaned and scaled

Fine sea salt and freshly ground black pepper

2 tablespoons chopped fresh parsley

SERVES 4

1. Preheat the oven to 400°F / 200°C. Line a baking sheet with parchment paper.

2. **Make the potatoes.** In a large bowl, toss the potatoes with the olive oil and salt and pepper to taste until evenly coated. Spread the potatoes out in a single layer on the prepared baking sheet. Roast, flipping the potatoes halfway through, until golden brown and crispy, 20 to 25 minutes.

3. **Make the acqua pazza.** In a large sauté pan, heat the olive oil over medium heat. Add the garlic and onion and sauté until the garlic is fragrant and the onion is translucent, 3 to 4 minutes. Add the cherry tomatoes and cook until softened, 2 to 3 minutes. Pour in the wine and bring to a simmer. Cook until slightly reduced, about 2 minutes. Add the stock, lemon zest, and capers, then return to a simmer until the flavors have melded, 2 minutes.

4. Pat the fish dry and season all over and inside with salt and pepper. Gently nestle the fish in the broth. Cover and cook until the fish is opaque and flakes easily with a fork, about 15 minutes.

5. Arrange the roasted potatoes on a serving platter to make a bed for the fish. Place the fish on top.

6. Spoon the acqua pazza sauce over the fish and potatoes. Garnish with parsley and serve immediately.

Sea Bream all'Acqua Pazza
with Crispy Potatoes
page 121

POMODORI RIPIENI ALLA ROMANA

Roman Stuffed Tomatoes

I first had this dish on my honeymoon almost twenty years ago in Rome. My husband and I were seated next to a very kind older couple who seemed to be of some standing with the waiters—they all addressed the man as "professore" and catered to his every whim. He knew his food well, and when he noticed that we skipped all the antipasti and went straight to the carbonara, he told us we'd made a terrible mistake and ordered a few specialties for us to try. Among them were a vignarola (Plantia's spring vegetable stew) that I included in *French Country Cooking* and these very traditional rice-filled tomatoes on a bed of potatoes that were his favorite. So now both of Il Professore's favorite recipes are in my books. Some serendipitous meetings are more flavorful than others.

4 beefsteak tomatoes (each about 8 ounces / 250 g)

1 medium yellow onion, peeled and coarsely chopped

1 garlic clove, minced

Fine sea salt and freshly ground black pepper

4 fresh basil leaves

3 teaspoons dried oregano

5 tablespoons / 75 ml extra-virgin olive oil, plus more for drizzling

½ cup / 50 g grated Pecorino Romano cheese

⅔ cup / 120 g carnaroli rice

1 pound / 450 g Yukon Gold potatoes, peeled and cut into 1-inch / 2.5 cm cubes

2 tablespoons / 15 g dried breadcrumbs

SERVES 4

1. Preheat the oven to 350°F / 180°C.

2. Slice the tops off the tomatoes using a very sharp knife and reserve. Carefully scoop out the insides, discarding the seeds but reserving the pulp. Turn the tomatoes upside down to allow any excess liquid to drain out.

3. In a blender, combine the tomato pulp, onion, garlic, and salt and pepper to taste and blend until smooth, 2 to 3 minutes. Add the basil and blend for another 30 seconds. Transfer to a large bowl and add 1½ teaspoons of the oregano, a drizzle of olive oil, the Pecorino Romano, and rice. Cover and let the mixture rest for an hour.

4. In a large baking dish, toss the potatoes with 3 tablespoons of the olive oil, salt and pepper to taste, the breadcrumbs, and the remaining 1½ teaspoons oregano.

5. Place the tomatoes on top of the potatoes, then fill with the rice mixture. Place the tomato caps on top of each stuffed tomato and drizzle with the remaining 2 tablespoons olive oil. Loosely cover the baking sheet with foil and bake until the tomatoes are tender and the rice is cooked through, about 1 hour and 10 minutes.

6. Preheat the broiler. Remove the foil from the tomatoes and slide the tomato caps to the side. Place the baking sheet 4 to 6 inches / 10 to 15 cm under the broiler and broil until the rice is lightly charred, about 5 minutes (watch carefully).

7. Let cool for 15 minutes, put the caps back on the tomatoes, and serve with the potatoes on the side.

TIMBALLO DI MELANZANE

Eggplant Pasta Cake

This is another one of those layered dishes that I so love. It's so fun (and sometimes scary) to unmold and very exciting to serve to guests. Slicing into any dish made in this way is like carving a cake; the ingredients may be simple, but the outcome is nothing less than elevated and ceremonial.

Timballos (or timpanos) are made in various ways throughout Italy. This version, a cousin of the parmigiana, comes from the southern region of Campania, and while it's wonderful as a starter, I think it can be a great main course on its own. The name, timballo, refers to both the dish and the cylindrical (drumlike) pot used for cooking it. The tube springform pan used here makes it easier to unmold without having to distort the beautiful timballo. To me, this is one of the most iconic Italian dishes, and when I make this at home for my family, it makes me feel like a real Italian mamma.

5 tablespoons / 75 ml extra-virgin olive oil, plus more as needed

1 garlic clove, minced

3¼ cups / 750 ml tomato passata

A few fresh basil leaves

Fine sea salt

2 globe eggplants, sliced into ¼-inch / 6 mm thick pieces

1 pound / 500 g dried short pasta of your choice (I like to use maccheroni)

½ cup / 50 g grated Parmigiano Reggiano cheese

1 cup / 150 g diced caciocavallo or provolone cheese

¾ cup / 100 g diced fresh mozzarella cheese

SERVES 6

1. Preheat the oven to 400°F / 200°C.

2. In a sauté pan, heat 1 tablespoon of the olive oil over medium heat. Add the garlic and sauté until golden, 2 minutes. Add the passata and cook, stirring occasionally, until it simmers, about 15 minutes. Add the basil, season with salt, and remove the pan from the heat.

3. Line a plate with paper towels. In a large skillet, heat the remaining 4 tablespoons / 60 ml olive oil over medium heat. Working in batches, fry the eggplant until golden, about 2 minutes per side. Transfer to the paper towel–lined plate to drain. Repeat with the remaining eggplant, adding more oil as needed.

4. Bring a large pot of salted water to a boil over high heat. Add the pasta and cook to al dente according to the package directions. Drain the pasta and add to the pot with the tomato sauce, then stir in the cheeses.

5. Line the bottom and sides of an 11-inch / 28 cm tube springform pan with the fried eggplant, overlapping slightly. Transfer the pasta to the eggplant-lined pan, spreading it evenly. Bake until golden, about 30 minutes. Let cool for about 5 minutes. Place a large platter over the pan and, in a swift motion and using a pot holder under the warm pan, flip the pan onto the platter. Carefully release the tube springform pan and unmold the pasta. Serve immediately.

VEAL PIZZAIOLA

Alla pizzaiola means "pizza style," so any meat cooked like this is topped with tomato sauce and herbs, usually oregano or basil. This manner of cooking is very common in the South and was historically a clever way of bringing out the best from the lesser cuts of meat; the theory being that any meat tastes better when served with tomatoes. My kids couldn't agree more. This is another family favorite, and I usually make it with thinly sliced veal scaloppine, which go well with anything (including the lemon version on page 54). Serve with sautéed spinach, slightly spicy, and roast potatoes with garlic and rosemary on the side to soak up the sauce.

1 pound / 500 g thinly sliced veal loin

Fine sea salt and freshly ground black pepper

5 tablespoons / 75 ml extra-virgin olive oil

2 garlic cloves, thinly sliced

12 ounces / 400 g canned peeled tomatoes, seeded and chopped

A handful of fresh parsley, chopped, plus more for garnish

2 tablespoons chopped fresh oregano, or 1 teaspoon dried

2 tablespoons / 15 grams capers (optional), for garnish

SERVES 4

1. Season the veal all over with salt.

2. In a large skillet, heat the olive oil over medium heat. Add the garlic and cook until golden, 2 minutes. Add the veal and cook, turning occasionally, until golden, about 2 minutes on each side. Transfer the veal to a plate and cover with foil to keep warm.

3. To the same pan, add the tomatoes, parsley, and oregano. Reduce the heat to low and cook, stirring occasionally, until the tomatoes break down and become saucy, about 15 minutes. Add the veal and any juices to the sauce. Season with salt and pepper and cook until warmed through, about 1 minute.

4. Sprinkle with more parsley, scatter with capers (if using), and serve immediately.

The Table

If there is a cornerstone in our lives, one thing that, more than anything, makes us who we are as a family, it's the table. Every night for dinner, and most weekends for lunch as well, we have a meal together at our dining table— sometimes in the kitchen and sometimes in the dining room. Usually one of the kids sets the table; another lights the candles. After dinner we take turns doing dishes, and someone has to walk the dogs. We would never consider spending our evenings any other way—for us it's unthinkable to eat separately, to eat different foods or at different times.

There was no grand design to live like this; our dedication to the table just happened. It's not like we discussed and decided, based on research, that this way of life was for the best. But I think it is.

I love to cook, so that's step number one. In fact, Oddur and I both love to cook, and we alternate our roles, though people often assume I do all the cooking (I just do most of it), which is helpful as well. Add the fact that we lived in the countryside for so long, and frankly, shopping for food, then cooking it and enjoying the results by candlelight is just about as exciting as a Friday night gets in a remote corner of France. My mother, when she visited us for the first time, said, in her thick French accent, "How can you live in this place? To be able to stand it you have to be an alcoholic." I don't quite agree, but I see her point. Luckily, we love to eat even more than we like to drink.

We brought this way of life back with us to the city when we moved to Turin, and like some people coming out of a time machine from another age, we were shocked to find that not everyone else does the same. The family unit is strong in Italy, and most Italian families share a few meals together every week, especially on Sundays. But modern times and changing habits are catching up with Italian families as well, albeit at a slower pace than in most other cultures.

Friends from other countries "practice the table" even less, and it's not uncommon to meet people who hardly ever eat with their families, or if they do, it's a fleeting affair. They work long hours and don't have time or are exhausted, their little kids are picky eaters, the teenagers can't be bothered or are never home. And besides, they'd rather run a bath and eat in front of a movie than go through all that work.

I understand all that, and the last thing I want to do is tell people how to live. There is no one formula for a well-lived life. I can only share my own experience and what it means to me. Yes, sometimes I'd rather run a bath myself and not have to cook. That's when my husband steps up. Sometimes we order in. But we lay it on the table; we take that brief moment to dine together. It's second nature to the family, but there are obstacles. (One of the enemies of the table is "the teenager," and another is screen time.)

Sometimes these meals make me crazy, and there are days when I'm standing in the kitchen alone doing dishes, when everyone else had to rush off for something more "important." A meal that took so long to make was over so fast, there was no real appreciation for the food, and the dinner was unpleasant because someone was fighting or my husband was telling the kids off a little too harshly. Those nights are the exceptions, but they happen. The next day we are back to discussing what to have for dinner, who will cook it, what to get.

There is great pleasure in cooking a delicious meal and sharing it with the family. When we hit the high notes, we go really high. If we didn't have the table, I feel I would know my children less. We are all so busy, or maybe just preoccupied. The table allows for conversation and gives everyone a platform to be heard. It can also bring drama (my husband gives no discounts on manners). The table is not a fairy tale, but it's a constant, an anchor, and a bond that ties us together. To put it very bluntly: Why bother having children if you're not going to try to spend time with them, get to know them properly, participate in their ups and downs? There are other ways to do this that don't include food, but food is my medium and the table is our way.

When we invite friends for dinner they often ask, "Do you always eat like this?" They mean the whole package, all the homemade food, the setting, the wine, the candles. We are no longer surprised at the question, but at the heart of it, fundamentally, is a reflection of a changing world. A few decades ago nobody would have asked, but these days, the table is gathering dust in many homes.

As human beings, we have made great progress in many areas. There is more tolerance; people can typically speak more openly than they ever did, about anything. But you need a place to say it. The table is perfect for that.

THE STORY OF *OUR* TABLE

I'm not particularly attached to things. I've learned over time that most possessions can be replaced, that memories created over meals with friends and family are far more valuable than the chairs we sat on or the porcelain plates that held our food, however precious. Our kitchen table might be the exception. It has become symbolic. Let me tell you the story of *the* table.

We bought our home in France from a man whose mother had lived and died in the house. After her death, some years before, he had sold much of the contents of the interior to local antique dealers and waited for the house to find a buyer at a price he could accept. He was a nice man named Jean-Claude, and we got to know him a bit. When we started the renovations on the kitchen, one of the first things we needed was a kitchen table. After searching for a few days, we found a simple oak table hiding in a corner at one of the many local brocantes in our region. It was the right size to fit the kitchen and seat our family, and while other tables were more obviously beautiful than this one, worn and wounded with three drawers on one side, it was the one for us. The kitchen finally got into shape, the cooking carousel began, and as we had no other table in the house, every meal was had in the kitchen in those early days. Some weeks later, we invited Jean-Claude to a dinner in his childhood home. When he entered the kitchen, he nearly fell to the floor. The table we bought had always been in our kitchen until he sold it to the brocante where we later found it.

I always believed that the table belonged to the house, and we left it there when we moved to Turin. But now that we are selling the house, I've changed my mind. The table belongs to my family. A new owner might not share our taste and could discard the table like Jean-Claude did. So the table came to our new home in Italy. We sent our eldest son, Thorir, to retrieve it and a few other things. Seeing the table again after a few years was like finding your dog after he's run away from home and gotten lost in the woods. It seemed smaller somehow; it was cowed, dusty, and gray—the years of solitude and humidity hadn't been kind. We gave it some love, applied some wax and a touch of color, and now it's our kitchen table in Turin. Not as good as new but something better, old with scars and ready to serve. Its fissures are clogged with flour from pasta making. It has been covered and soaked in every liquid used in cooking and some that are not. It's a good table, it's our table. And we will never ever sell it.

MOUSSE DI FRAGOLE

Strawberry Mousse

We get Italian strawberries as early as March (mostly from Basilicata), but they are, along with peaches and plums, the fruits I connect most with summer. I get a bit lazy with making elaborate desserts when temperatures rise; some fresh fruit or the endless selection of gelato available to us usually does the trick. When I'm in the mood, though, for a special occasion or special guests, this light and delicious strawberry mousse is an elegant way to end a summer meal. Just thinking about it now brings me back to breezy alfresco dinners, long tables, and garden lights.

3 cups / 450 g strawberries, stems removed and quartered, plus more for garnish

⅓ cup / 65 g superfine sugar

1 tablespoon unflavored gelatin powder

3 cups / 700 ml heavy cream

SERVES 8

1. In a large bowl, toss the strawberries with the sugar until coated.

2. Transfer the strawberries to a food processor and pulse until smooth. Strain the puree through a fine-mesh sieve into a large bowl.

3. In a small saucepan, combine ¼ cup / 50 g of the strawberry puree and the gelatin. Cook over low heat, stirring constantly, until the gelatin completely dissolves. Whisk the mixture into the remaining strawberry puree until combined.

4. In a large bowl, use a hand mixer with a whisk attachment to whip the cream until soft peaks form, then fold a quarter of the whipped cream into the strawberry mixture. Use a rubber spatula to fold in the remaining whipped cream until well combined.

5. Divide the mousse between 8 coupe glasses and refrigerate for at least 4 hours, or until set. Garnish with strawberries before serving.

TORTA PARADISO

Italians tend to have sweet things for breakfast, such as cornettos (or croissants) filled with jam or pastry creams, even chocolate. What I usually prefer is really good toast—preferably sourdough—with butter, and maybe an egg, plus a cup of strong tea (I grew up in a British colony after all). But if I have something sweet for breakfast, it would be along the lines of this cake. One theory about this sugary breakfast tradition is that Italian food on the whole is so rich, varied, and delicious—people are feasting all the time and often at a late hour—that all they need in the morning is a shot of espresso and a little pastry. By contrast, the English, traditionally, eat earlier at night and (according to the Italians) much worse. Which explains why they need something more substantial (think of the traditional English breakfast with all the fixings) to get them going in the morning. Who knows? Let's just call it different approaches.

The cake in question got its name because apparently once upon a time a wealthy countess declared, "This cake is paradise." Usually I don't make this cake for breakfast per se; it's lovely to have after a rich dinner, maybe with some seasonal fruits or berries on the side. Regardless of when you enjoy it, it really is the perfect sponge cake, so finely balanced, and goes well with coffee or tea.

8 tablespoons / 115 g unsalted butter, at room temperature, plus more for greasing the pan

⅔ cup / 130 g superfine sugar

⅔ cup / 80 g all-purpose flour

⅔ cup / 80 g cornstarch

1 teaspoon baking powder

2 large egg yolks

2 large eggs

¾ cup plus 2 tablespoons / 200 ml heavy cream

1 tablespoon powdered sugar

1 tablespoon honey

SERVES 6

1. Preheat the oven to 350°F / 175°C. Butter and flour a 9-inch / 23 cm cake pan.

2. In a medium bowl, beat the butter with the superfine sugar. Sift in the flour, cornstarch, and baking powder, then add the egg yolks and eggs. Mix with a spatula until combined.

3. Pour the batter into the prepared cake pan. Bake until golden, 25 to 30 minutes. Let cool completely in the pan and unmold.

4. In a large bowl, use a hand mixer with a whisk attachment to whip the cream with the powdered sugar until soft peaks form. Once whipped, fold in the honey.

5. Spread the cream on top of the cake and serve.

To Live by the Eye

by Oddur Thorisson

I am a photographer by profession, but it sometimes feels that my real work is arranging vegetables for a living, and for sport. I'm joking, of course, but only half. I never expected to spend much of my time photographing food. I fell into it, largely thanks to my wife, whose book this is.

I have always loved beautiful things, well-made things. *Craftsmanship* is the word, and nobody crafts better stuff than nature. The hue of a chestnut. A beautiful tree. A cabbage whose leaves create a wonderful, contrasted maze of shadows and light. Long before I started taking pictures for cookbooks, I began arranging vegetables in my own house, just to look at.

The celebrated photographer Henri Cartier-Bresson—who lived by the eye—was interviewed once in his retirement. "Do you not take pictures anymore, Mr. Bresson?" he was asked. "I do," he answered. "I just took one of you now, with my eyes. You don't need a camera to take photos."

I always enjoyed that story because it's insightful and true and was told by a master. You don't need a camera, but it helps to have something interesting in front of you. In my younger years, I was inspired by beautiful restaurants in France and Italy that displayed an abundance of seasonal fruits and vegetables. (The mountain of apricots and cherries at L'Amis Louis in Paris in May comes to mind. I took a picture of that one with my eyes many years ago; I'm looking at it now.)

I started replicating these installations at home. Local greengrocers thought I ran a restaurant. "He's so particular about what he buys," they said. Soon after, they began putting unusual specimens aside for me, a tomato that looked like a clown, an orange that looked like a snowman. But I was more interested in the regular stuff. An onion that looks like an onion. Abundance became our calling card, and luckily we had so many kids that nothing went to waste. When Mimi had her cooking show in France, *La Table de Mimi*, the film crew took over our house and bought the necessary ingredients. One recipe had five peaches. So they bought five peaches. "You don't understand," I said. "To use five peaches you need fifty." They shook their heads. "We don't have a budget for that." Then they added, "What will you do with fifty peaches?"

"Look at them," I whispered to myself, then I drove to the market and bought fifty peaches. (This was in summer, when a crate of peaches in France is almost free.)

Soon after, we were invited to a beautiful country house in Gascony. Our friend showed us the kitchens and proclaimed, "We're doing a Mimi and Oddur." They had done a vegetable installation, a beautiful one. She said that they had always been storing vegetables in the pantry, but we had inspired them to bring them out.

It's normal to put flowers proudly on display, but food, to most people, has only one function and must be hidden until it's chopped and fried. The very banal fruit bowl, often with five peaches, is an exception, and eggs sometimes get a bit of play on the counter. A bowl of nuts is an accepted Christmas classic.

All foods are better bought in something that resembles their original form. A whole chicken is a beautiful thing; a few pale breasts under a layer of plastic are not. A bunch of carrots from the market can be gorgeous; put them in a ziplock and they look like they're intended for astronauts.

Yes, most food generally stores better in the fridge. But plenty of produce does not. Admittedly, this approach requires a bit more thought and maintenance, but vegetables can be just as beautiful to look at as flowers.

They say that people who worry suffer twice and I agree. But you can flip that thought and enjoy things twice. Isn't it a nice thought that, when you buy your onions and leeks and lemons, you can enjoy them twice? You will savor having them on your plate, but why not enjoy them a little first? By the eye.

Autunno / Autumn

Antipasti

Primi

Secondi

Dolci

POLENTA CAKE *with* SAGE & SHALLOTS

We are a large family with many friends, so it's not uncommon for someone to pop in unexpectedly for one reason or another. I like to offer something homemade to my guests, even if they are unannounced. This savory polenta cake is my go-to, easy to whip up quickly but with heartwarming results. We have an abundance of sage on our terrace, and I always have the other ingredients in my cupboards. Either I sneak into the kitchen and slide the cake into the oven or the guests follow me and we continue our conversation over tea or a glass of wine while I put this recipe together. Now the "problem" is that unexpected guests come especially for the cake, so I'm under pressure to make it or something similar every time.

It also works very well as a part of a picnic meal, served alongside salads and fruits.

¾ cup / 180 ml extra-virgin olive oil, plus more for greasing the pan

4 shallots, finely chopped

½ cup plus 1 tablespoon / 20 g chopped fresh sage

1 cup / 170 g ground polenta

1 cup / 100 g dried breadcrumbs

¾ cup / 110 g all-purpose flour, sifted

1 tablespoon baking powder

1 tablespoon granulated sugar

1 cup / 100 g grated Parmigiano Reggiano cheese

1 teaspoon fine sea salt and 1 teaspoon freshly ground black pepper

2 large eggs, beaten

1 cup / 250 ml whole milk

SERVES 6

1. Preheat the oven to 400°F / 200°C. Grease an 8-inch / 20 cm cake pan with olive oil.

2. In a medium skillet, heat 2 tablespoons of the olive oil over medium heat. Add the shallots and sage and sauté until golden, 8 minutes. Set aside.

3. In a large bowl, combine the polenta, breadcrumbs, flour, baking powder, sugar, Parmigiano Reggiano, salt, and pepper. In a medium bowl, combine the eggs, milk, and remaining 10 tablespoons / 150 ml olive oil. Fold the wet ingredients into the polenta mixture, then fold in the sautéed shallots and sage. Pour the batter into the prepared cake pan.

4. Bake until golden and a toothpick inserted into the center comes out clean, 20 to 25 minutes. Let cool for 10 minutes before unmolding. Serve warm.

STAUB

PEPPERS STUFFED *with* CHEESE & HAM

We are very spoiled in Italy when it comes to produce. This is really the land where beautiful food grows in abundance. Seasonal cooking is a little bit more elastic here than in many other places since the window for each fruit or vegetable tends to be longer and more bountiful. Peppers are available throughout summer, but I find them at their delicious best in autumn, especially here in Piemonte, where the famous peperone di Carmagnola are at their peak in September and October. I first had a version of this dish at one of our favorite restaurants in Napoli, Mimì alla Ferrovia, many years ago. We always include these peppers in the antipasti we order when we go there; anything else would be unthinkable.

These are subtle flavors rather than spicy, but oh so delicious, rustic, and elegant at the same time.

Filling

1 cup / 110 g stale bread pieces, crusts removed

10 ounces / 300 g fresh mozzarella cheese, diced

2 ounces / 60 g caciocavallo di bufala or provolone cheese, diced

1 ounce / 30 g grated Parmigiano Reggiano cheese

2 ounces / 60 g cooked ham, diced

Fine sea salt and freshly ground black pepper

1 large egg, beaten

10 small red bell peppers (about 2 pounds / 1 kg)

Extra-virgin olive oil, for drizzling and greasing the pan

6 tablespoons / 45 g dried breadcrumbs

SERVES 6 (ABOUT 16 ROLLS)

1. **Make the filling.** In a small bowl, soak the bread in water until softened, then squeeze out the water and crumble into small pieces.

2. In a medium bowl, combine the cheeses, ham, soaked bread, a pinch of salt and pepper, and half of the beaten egg. Mix until the mixture is well combined, like a thick, coarse paste. Chill in the refrigerator for at least 1 hour to firm up the mixture.

3. Meanwhile, roast the peppers directly over a gas flame or under the broiler. Turn occasionally, until charred all over, about 10 minutes. Transfer to a large bowl, cover tightly with plastic wrap, and let steam for 15 minutes. When cool enough to handle, peel and seed the peppers, pat them dry, and cut them lengthwise into 2-inch / 5 cm wide strips.

4. Preheat the oven to 325°F / 160°C.

5. Grease a 9 × 13 inch / 23 × 33 cm baking pan with olive oil. Place 3 tablespoons / 40 g of filling on each pepper strip, then roll the pepper tightly. Arrange the rolled pepper strips neatly in the baking pan. Sprinkle with breadcrumbs and drizzle all over with olive oil.

6. Bake until golden, about 30 minutes. Let cool for 10 minutes before serving.

MACCHERONI PASTA FRITTERS

We like to call all sorts of food decadent, particularly creamy desserts, but also foods that are deep-fried, cheesy, and rich. This little nugget may be the most wicked of all, for it includes all of the above. Pasta and cheese mixed together, covered with breadcrumbs, and deep-fried to deliciousness.

Real Neapolitan pizzerias tend to offer nothing but pizza, so asking for a salad or a vegetable side dish will have the waiter either scratching their head or shaking it in disbelief. It is, however, customary to start the meal with something fried, whether it be croquettes, Roman supplì, Sicilian arancini, or these fried pasta fritters. My rule of thumb when serving pasta fritters to guests or the family: one per person. Basta.

1 pound / 500 g dried maccheroni or any short tube pasta

2 tablespoons extra-virgin olive oil

5 ounces / 150 g cooked ham, diced

1 garlic clove, crushed

½ cup / 70 g green peas, fresh or thawed if frozen

¼ cup / 25 g grated Parmigiano Reggiano cheese

1½ to 1¾ cups / 350 to 400 ml Béchamel, cooled (page 98)

Fine sea salt and freshly ground black pepper

1 cup plus 7 tablespoons/ 225 g all-purpose flour

2 cups / 200 g dried breadcrumbs, for dredging

Vegetable oil, for frying

MAKES 15 FRITTERS

1. Bring a large pot of salted water to a boil over high heat. Add the pasta and cook to al dente according to the package directions. Drain and set aside.

2. In a medium skillet, heat the olive oil over medium heat. Add the ham, garlic, and peas and sauté until lightly browned and fragrant, about 3 minutes. Discard the garlic. Let cool for 5 minutes.

3. In a large bowl, combine the ham mixture, pasta, Parmigiano Reggiano, béchamel, and salt and pepper to taste. Spread a large sheet (about 26 inches / 65 cm) of parchment paper on your work surface and pour the mixture onto it. Shape the mixture into a roll about 20 inches / 50 cm long. Wrap the parchment paper tightly around the roll, sealing the ends securely. Place the roll in the refrigerator and let it firm up for at least 1 hour.

4. Remove the roll from the refrigerator and cut it into 15 rounds, each about 1¼ inches / 3 cm thick. If necessary, you can reshape them with your hands to restore their circular shape.

5. To prepare the batter, in a medium bowl, combine 2 cups / 500 ml cold water with the flour and whisk until the mixture is smooth and free of lumps. Place the breadcrumbs in a shallow bowl. Line a baking sheet with parchment paper. Dip each patty into the batter, allowing the excess to drain off, then coat in breadcrumbs. Ensure the patties are evenly coated and place them on the prepared baking sheet.

6. Line a plate with paper towels. Pour about 1 inch / 2.5 cm oil into a large, high-sided pan. Heat the oil to about 375°F / 190°C over medium heat. You can test whether the oil is hot enough by adding in a small drop of batter. If it sizzles and turns golden and crisp, the oil is ready.

7. Working in batches, fry the patties until golden brown, a few minutes per side, then transfer them to the paper towel–lined plate to drain. Let cool and serve.

ZINGARA ISCHITANA

Sandwich with Prosciutto, Mozzarella & Tomato

Italian cuisine has conquered the world, and it's perhaps logical or at least understandable that we tend to think of the most famous dishes as having existed forever, or at least for a very long time. The truth is that many of the greatest hits of Italian cuisine are much more recent than one would imagine. The Romans were not feasting on pasta with tomato sauce, nor were the Medicis of Florence. The tomato only found its way to Italy in the mid-1500s and rose to culinary prominence in the nineteenth century. The famous carbonara pasta from Rome was born only in the mid-twentieth century, and so forth.

In the same period, the Zingara story goes that free spirits (call them hippies) started selling a delicious sandwich near the port of Ischia, a predecessor of street food. The trend caught on, and soon the sandwich was made all over the island. Now it's the pride of Ischia in gastronomic terms. The name Zingara is a nod to its free-spirited origins and the era. And while you may think, "This is just a sandwich," you have to consider two things: A really good sandwich is never just a sandwich. And second, at the time, a sandwich like this would have been hard to find in Italy (or anywhere). The quality of the ham, the wonderful mozzarella, the sourdough, all crunchy and melted together. You want one now, don't you?

1 medium heirloom tomato, thickly sliced

Extra-virgin olive oil

Fine sea salt and freshly ground black pepper

2 large slices crusty bread (like sourdough)

2 tablespoons mayonnaise

Pinch of dried oregano

A few leaves of lettuce

2 slices fresh mozzarella cheese

3 ounces / 70 g Prosciutto di Carpegna (or your favorite cured ham)

SERVES 1

1. Season the tomato with the olive oil, salt, and pepper.

2. Toast the bread lightly.

3. Spread the mayonnaise in an even layer on the cut sides of the bread. Top one slice with the seasoned tomato, oregano, lettuce, mozzarella, and prosciutto. Top with the other slice of bread.

4. Drizzle the outside layers of the bread with olive oil. Heat a nonstick or cast-iron skillet over medium-high heat for a minute or two. If you're unsure whether the pan is hot enough, sprinkle a few drops of water in the pan; if the water sizzles and evaporates, it's ready.

5. Carefully place the sandwich in the hot pan and cook until the bread turns golden and crisp, 2 to 3 minutes on each side. Press gently on the sandwich with a spatula to help it toast evenly. Once both sides are golden and the cheese is melted, remove from the pan.

6. Let cool for a minute before slicing in half diagonally. Serve immediately while it's still warm and crispy.

POTATO CROQUETTES

These stuffed potato balls, rolled in breadcrumbs, then deep-fried, are as Neapolitan as pizza. Locally, they are known simply as crocchè, and Neapolitans munch on them all day—before a meal, as a light snack, or with their aperitivo in the early evening. Many people probably associate potato croquettes chiefly with Spanish tapas traditions, but they are just as prevalent in Campania as they are in Spain. This might have to do with the fact that Naples and Sicily were ruled for centuries by the Bourbons, the Spanish royal family. (There are mentions that croquettes may have been brought to Naples by the French, but I like the Bourbon explanation better.) This is a dish I make most often when I have leftover mashed potatoes from the night before. The family might even abstain from having a second portion of mash just in the hope of me making these the following day.

2 pounds / 1 kg russet potatoes

5 large eggs

1 cup / 100 g grated Parmigiano Reggiano cheese

Pinch of ground nutmeg

1 tablespoon finely chopped fresh parsley

1 teaspoon fine sea salt and 1 teaspoon freshly ground black pepper

4 ounces / 110 g mortadella or cooked ham, diced

½ cup / 60 g all-purpose flour

2 cups / 200 g dried breadcrumbs

Vegetable oil, for frying

SERVES 4 TO 6

1. Place the potatoes in a large pot of salted water. Bring to a boil over medium-high heat and cook until very tender, about 30 minutes. Let the potatoes cool for 10 minutes, then peel.

2. Place the potatoes in a ricer and rice them into a large bowl. Add 2 of the eggs, the Parmigiano Reggiano, nutmeg, parsley, salt, and pepper and mix until you get a stiff dough.

3. Roll a small, bite-size ball of dough (about 2 inches / 5 cm) and insert the mortadella, shaping the dough around it. Repeat until you have 20 to 25 croquettes.

4. Place the flour in one shallow bowl and the breadcrumbs in another. In a third shallow bowl, beat the remaining 3 eggs with a tablespoon of water. Dredge each croquette in the flour, then dip in the egg. Coat in the breadcrumbs and transfer to a plate. Once all the croquettes are breaded, chill in the refrigerator for an hour to firm up.

5. Line a plate with paper towels. Pour about 1 inch / 2.5 cm oil into a large, high-sided pan. Heat the oil to about 375°F / 190°C over medium-high heat. You can test whether the oil is hot enough by adding a small drop of batter. If it sizzles and turns golden and crisp, the oil is ready. Working in batches, fry the croquettes until golden brown all over, 3 to 5 minutes, then transfer to the paper towel–lined plate to drain. Let cool and serve.

GATTÒ

Neapolitan Potato Cake

We spend our summers on the island of Procida, and on one of my first visits (I'm always keen to know more about local foods, insider tips), I asked a taxi driver what his favorite dish was. Gattò, he said. I confessed I'd never heard about it. So he told me at length, like a true Neapolitan, how wonderful it is, how delicious and satisfying and tasty. His declaration of love for the gattò lasted the whole ride. Soon after, I asked another taxi driver the same question and he said, you guessed it, gattò. "Here we go again," I thought.

After that I had no choice but to try a gattò, then make it at home. Of course everyone loved it. I have always enjoyed a French potato cake with too much garlic and butter as a side dish for a good steak or duck breast, but this Italian version is either a meal on its own or a great way to start one (as long as the slice is not too large). It's like a cousin of the spaghetti cake earlier in the book (page 93), but with potatoes rather than pasta.

½ cup / 50 g dried breadcrumbs

3 pounds / 1.5 kg russet potatoes (6 to 7 medium potatoes), peeled

7 tablespoons / 100 g unsalted butter, plus more for greasing the pan

1 cup / 100 g grated Parmigiano Reggiano cheese

½ cup / 50 g grated Pecorino Romano cheese

3 large eggs

1 large egg yolk

3½ ounces / 100 g Neapolitan salami or Parma ham, cubed

¼ cup finely chopped fresh parsley

Fine sea salt and freshly ground black pepper

¼ cup / 60 ml whole milk

3½ ounces / 100 g fresh mozzarella cheese, sliced

3½ ounces / 100 g smoked scamorza cheese, sliced

3½ ounces / 100 g mortadella, cubed

3 hard-boiled eggs, coarsely chopped

SERVES 6

1. Preheat the oven to 350°F / 180°C. Grease a 9-inch / 23 cm springform pan with butter and coat with half of the breadcrumbs.

2. Place the potatoes in a large pot of salted water. Bring to a boil over medium-high heat and cook until very tender, about 30 minutes. Drain and mash them with a potato masher in the same pot. Add the butter, Parmigiano Reggiano, Pecorino Romano, eggs and egg yolk, salami, parsley, 1 teaspoon salt, 1 teaspoon pepper, and the milk and mix with a fork until well combined. Transfer half the mixture to the prepared springform pan and press into the bottom and sides.

3. Scatter the mozzarella, scamorza, mortadella, and hard-boiled eggs over the potato mixture and season with salt and pepper to taste. Cover with the remaining potato mixture and sprinkle with the remaining breadcrumbs.

4. Bake until the gattò is browned and bubbling, 45 minutes. Remove from the oven, cover, and let cool. Unmold onto a serving plate and serve immediately.

FREGOLA SARDA *with* MUSSELS *in* TOMATO BROTH

Italy has twenty regions, and I've been to nineteen, most of them repeatedly. The one region I've never visited is Sardinia, and it's a wrong I must right. Food, though, can take you places; it allows you to travel where you've never been. When we lived in Paris—before you could easily get a good pizza in every neighborhood or even source zucchini flowers, radicchio, or a guanciale for your carbonara—the only truly good Italian restaurant in town was Sardinian. We went there often and had delicious suckling pig, pasta with sea urchin or bottarga, and the fregola sarda, perhaps the most Sardinian dish of all. I've been making it at home for almost twenty years now, and it remains a family favorite.

I make a fregola only when I can find very good, very fresh mussels (to paraphrase a quote from Oscar Wilde, the only way to behave with mussels is to buy them when they are extra fresh and to buy something else when they are not). Many versions of this dish are a little dry for my taste, almost like a Sicilian couscous. I like to serve mine on the soupy side, with plenty of broth, so you'll need a spoon. This is a perfect kitchen party dish, a complete meal with lots of good bread on the side and good Sardinian white wine.

3 pounds / 1.5 kg mussels

1 cup / 250 ml dry white wine

Pinch of saffron

3 tablespoons extra-virgin olive oil, plus more for serving

1 small onion, thinly sliced

1 garlic clove, thinly sliced

14 ounces / 400 g canned peeled tomatoes

A bunch of fresh parsley, finely chopped

2 cups / 500 ml hot vegetable stock

8 ounces / 250 g fregola sarda

½ teaspoon crushed red pepper flakes

Fine sea salt and freshly ground black pepper

SERVES 4

1. Clean the mussels in several water baths. Scrub their shells and pull off their beards. Fill a large bowl or pot with salted water and add the mussels. Let stand for at least 1 hour to eliminate the sand. Drain the mussels and rinse several times until there is no more sand. Scrub again if necessary.

2. Add the mussels to a large pot and pour in the wine. Cover and cook, stirring occasionally, over medium heat until the mussels open, 3 to 5 minutes. Strain the mussel broth into a large bowl. Add the saffron to the warm liquid. Set aside.

3. In a separate large pot, heat the olive oil over medium heat. Once the oil is glistening, add the onion and garlic and sauté until softened, 4 minutes. Add the tomatoes, half of the parsley, the hot vegetable stock, and mussel broth and stir to combine. Bring to a gentle boil and add the fregola sarda. Simmer until the pasta is al dente, 10 to 12 minutes.

4. Right before serving, add the mussels to the mixture. Drizzle with olive oil, season with pepper flakes, salt, and black pepper and garnish with the remaining parsley. Serve in individual soup bowls.

Servizio
Ristoranti
Piazza della Repubblica, 26 mercato 5°
cell. 335 7040425 - mail:

2021

TAGLIATELLE *with* BRA SAUSAGE, LEEKS & HAZELNUT RAGÙ

This recipe is my latest obsession. It wasn't even supposed to be in the book, and I didn't include it in the original recipe list or even the revised one. We have amazing leeks in Piemonte in the fall, just the best. Many of them come from Carmagnola, near Turin. Hazelnuts are one of Piemonte's most famous exports, and Bra sausage is the pride of local butchers. The sausage is mostly made from beef with a hint of pork fat, and it's so pure and good that it's eaten either raw or cooked; when served raw, it's often topped with a sprinkle of hazelnuts.

This pasta dish is a seasonal extension of that tradition. Tagliatelle is most often used for this recipe; its texture marries well with this chunky sauce.

I cooked it once in fall for a group of workshop guests because I wanted all the ingredients to be very local. We all loved it so much that they went home with hazelnuts and Bra sausage, and I cooked it the next day for my kids. I've probably made it eight times in as many weeks. That tells a story. I know that it's not always easy to source Bra sausage outside Piemonte, so I tried making the tagliatelle using regular sausage and the results were almost as yummy.

1 cup / 150 g hazelnuts, finely chopped

1 pound / 450 g Bra sausage (or a good-quality pork sausage)

5 tablespoons / 75 ml extra-virgin olive oil

6 medium leeks, white part thinly sliced

½ cup / 120 ml dry white wine

Fine sea salt and freshly ground black pepper

1 pound / 500 g dried tagliatelle pasta

2 tablespoons unsalted butter

½ cup / 50 g grated Parmigiano Reggiano cheese, for garnish

SERVES 4

1. In a medium sauté pan, toast the hazelnuts over medium heat until fragrant and golden, 5 to 6 minutes.

2. Remove the casings from the sausage and crumble the meat into bite-size pieces. In a large sauté pan, heat 2 tablespoons of the olive oil over medium heat. Add the sausage and cook until brown on all sides, 7 to 10 minutes. Once browned, remove the sausage from the pan and set aside.

3. To the same pan, add the remaining 3 tablespoons olive oil and the leeks. Sauté over medium heat until softened and slightly golden, 5 to 7 minutes.

4. Return the sausage to the pan with the leeks and toss everything together until all the flavors have melded. Pour in the wine, bring it to a simmer, and let it reduce by about half, 3 to 4 minutes. Season to taste with salt and pepper. Remove from the heat and set aside.

5. Bring a large pot of salted water to a boil over high heat. Add the pasta and cook until very al dente, 2 minutes less than the package directions (you will continue cooking it with the sausage and leeks). Reserving

recipe continues »

Tagliatelle with Bra Sausage, Leeks & Hazelnut Ragù CONTINUED

1 cup / 250 ml of the pasta water, drain the pasta.

6. Place the pan with the sausage and leek mixture over medium-high heat and add the butter. Stir until the butter has melted and add the pasta. Mix so that everything is well combined. If the mixture feels too dry, add a splash of the reserved pasta water to loosen it up. Add the toasted hazelnuts. Season with salt and pepper to taste. Serve immediately with Parmigiano Reggiano.

PASTA E PATATE

It's almost impossible to think of a more carb-loaded dish than this one, a starchy, spectacular stew of not only pasta but potatoes. In my fantasy, this is the dish they would serve me if I had been lost in the wilderness. After hours wandering in the cold, I would see a lit house in the far distance, smoke coming up the chimney. I would knock on the door and the family would invite me to join them at the table. They would place a huge pot in the middle of the table, and just the anticipation and a sip of simple wine would warm me up again. Maybe that's what heaven is like.

Extra-virgin olive oil

½ ounce / 15 g pancetta, diced

3½ ounces / 100 g celery, chopped

3½ ounces / 100 g carrots, chopped

1 medium onion, thinly sliced

5 medium russet potatoes, peeled and diced

5 cups / 1.2 liters vegetable stock

12 ounces / 320 g mixed small pasta (I like tubetti, ditalini, maccheroncini, and pasta mista)

1 cup / 100 g grated Parmigiano Reggiano cheese

½ cup / 50 g grated Pecorino Romano cheese

5 ounces / 150 g provola, mozzarella, or scamorza cheese, cubed and drained

A handful of fresh basil leaves, for garnish

Fine sea salt and freshly ground black pepper

SERVES 4

1. In a large pot, heat a drizzle of olive oil over medium heat. Add the pancetta and sauté until golden, 4 minutes. Add the celery, carrots, and onion and sauté until browned, 4 minutes more. Add the potatoes and cook until softened, another 5 minutes.

2. Add enough stock to cover the potatoes, bring to a boil, and reduce the heat to low. Cook until the potatoes are tender, about 10 minutes.

3. Add the remaining stock and the pasta to the pot. Continue cooking, stirring occasionally, until the pasta is al dente and has absorbed some of the stock, 10 to 12 minutes. If the pasta is too dry, add a bit of boiling water if needed, to keep a soupy consistency.

4. Once the pasta is ready, remove the pot from the heat. Stir in the cheeses and basil. Season with salt and pepper before serving.

ANELLETTI AL FORNO

Baked Pasta with Sicilian Ragù & Peas

I've said before that I have a great fondness for baked (al forno) dishes like timpano or lasagna—layered, often shapely delights. Every region of Italy has its favored pasta shapes and a way of doing things that differs slightly, or greatly, from other regions. Anelletti are ring-shaped pastas, native to the area around Palermo but spread all over Sicily. Every pasta shape gives a different sensation, and I love these rather unusual and round little wonders that dance on the palate.

We are a big family, so I usually make this dish for up to ten people. In such volume the easiest, most familial way to serve it is in a roasting pan like you would use for a lasagna. Then you dish out the portions with a large serving spoon. In restaurants in Sicily (or at home if you're only making it for two to four people), they often use a dome-shaped mold that looks very attractive and inviting on the plate once unmolded and served individually, much like a timpano.

Extra-virgin olive oil

½ cup / 50 g dried breadcrumbs

1 large onion, cut into small dice

2 carrots, cut into small dice

1 celery rib, cut into small dice

8 ounces / 250 g ground pork shoulder

10 ounces / 300 g ground beef

1 teaspoon fine sea salt

1 teaspoon freshly ground black pepper

1 cup / 250 ml red wine

1½ cups / 200 g frozen green peas

1 tablespoon tomato paste

3 cups / 700 g tomato puree

Vegetable oil, for frying

1 large eggplant, cut into 1-inch cubes

1 pound / 500 g dried anelletti pasta

7 ounces / 200 g various cold cuts (such as ham and salami), diced

7 ounces / 200 g caciocavallo or mozzarella cheese, diced

7 ounces / 200 g grated Parmigiano Reggiano cheese

SERVES 4 TO 6

1. Preheat the oven to 350°F / 180°C. Grease a 9 × 13-inch / 23 × 33 cm baking dish with olive oil, then sprinkle with 1 tablespoon of the breadcrumbs.

2. In a large saucepan, heat a drizzle of olive oil over medium heat. Add the onion, carrots, and celery and sauté until softened, 5 minutes. Add the pork, beef, salt, and pepper and sauté until browned, 5 minutes.

3. Add the wine, peas, tomato paste, tomato puree, and 1 quart / liter water. Cook, stirring occasionally, until you get a rich sauce, about 1 hour. If the sauce becomes too thick, stir in more water. Season with salt and pepper.

4. Line a plate with paper towels. Pour 1 inch / 2.5 cm of oil into a large, high-sided pan. Heat the oil to about 375°F / 190°C over medium heat. You can test if the oil is hot enough by dropping in a small piece of bread. If it turns golden brown immediately, the oil is ready. Working in batches, fry the eggplant cubes until browned, about 3 minutes. Transfer to the paper towel–lined plate to drain. Season with salt.

5. Bring a large pot of salted water to a boil over high heat. Add the pasta and cook until very al dente, 2 minutes less than the package directions. Drain the pasta, toss into the ragù, and mix gently to combine. Add the cold cuts, caciocavallo, and half of the Parmigiano Reggiano and mix well. Transfer to the prepared baking dish. Top with the remaining 3 tablespoons breadcrumbs and the Parmigiano Reggiano. Bake until golden and bubbling, 30 minutes. Let cool for 10 minutes before serving.

AGNOLOTTI PIEMONTESE

Piemontese cooking, just like Torino itself, might be described as the best-kept secret of Italian gastronomy. Emilian, Roman, and Neapolitan dishes are known everywhere and comprise what the world usually means when it speaks of "Italian food." Piemonte is not the land of tomatoes or eggplants, not the land of focaccia or pizza, or any type of fresh fish (Piemonte has no access to the sea, so the fish used in local dishes is always the canned type, anchovies or tuna). But here we have cream and eggs and meat galore, not to mention mushrooms, fresh pasta, hazelnuts, and chocolate. Piemonte has two types of traditional fresh pasta: tagliolini, which is usually served with a ragù, porcini, or truffles when in season (see page 177), and stuffed raviolis called agnolotti. Agnolotti exist in two different shapes: gobbo (typical, fairly large, square raviolis) and the smaller plin, which means "pinch" in the local dialect. The filling varies from family to family and village to village but invariably includes meat, and almost always more than one type.

This agnolotti, in the plin style, is a very traditional recipe, collected and adjusted by my good friend Claudia, who I like to call my Pasta Coach. She likes to serve this dish with a meat gravy as custom dictates. I use a mix of rabbit, beef, and pork, but you can just double up on the beef and omit the rabbit. Making traditional agnolotti is a laborious undertaking, but the results are endlessly rewarding. I recommend making this dish with friends or family, setting aside a part of the day when you can all come together, laugh, and cook. You'll need the pasta team, some on filling duty and at least one person to tend to the gravy. This is northern Italian family living.

Filling

4 tablespoons / 60 ml extra-virgin olive oil

7 ounces / 200 g rabbit, cut into 1-inch/ 3 cm cubes

7 ounces / 200 g beef, cut into 1-inch / 3 cm cubes

7 ounces / 200 g pork loin, cut into 1-inch / 3 cm cubes

1 leek, white part coarsely chopped

1 carrot, coarsely chopped

2 tablespoons chopped fresh parsley

1 teaspoon chopped fresh sage

1 teaspoon chopped fresh rosemary

1 cup / 250 ml red wine (such as Barolo or Barbaresco)

1 tablespoon fine sea salt

1 cup / 250 ml vegetable stock

1 large egg

2¼ cups / 200 g grated Parmigiano Reggiano cheese

1 teaspoon ground nutmeg

Ravioli Pasta Dough (recipe follows)

3 tablespoons / 40 g unsalted butter

SERVES 4 TO 6

1. In a large saucepan, heat the olive oil over medium heat. Add the rabbit, beef, and pork and cook until browned on all sides, 8 minutes. Add the leek, carrot, parsley, sage, and rosemary and cook, stirring, 5 minutes more. Add the wine and deglaze, stirring constantly. Season with the salt and scrape up all the browned bits. Add the stock and bring to a simmer. Reduce the heat to low, cover, and cook until the meat is tender, about 3 hours, adding water if dry.

2. Strain the braising liquid into a medium saucepan and set the meat mixture aside to cool. Cook the liquid over low heat until reduced and glossy, about 10 minutes. Set aside.

3. Once the meat mixture is cooled, transfer it to a food processor and pulse until a semicoarse paste forms. Transfer to a medium bowl. Add the egg, Parmigiano Reggiano, and nutmeg and mix with your hands

recipe continues »

Agnolotti Piemontese CONTINUED

until well combined. Chill for at least 30 minutes to firm up the mixture.

4. Lay out a rectangular pasta sheet and cut into strips about 3 inches / 7.5 cm wide. Place a line of hazelnut-size balls of filling about ¾-inch / 2 cm apart. Bring one edge of the dough over the filling and join it to the other edge, pressing both edges together, to create a long tube with little bulges of filling. With your thumb and forefinger, gently pinch the dough between each mound of filling to form distinct pockets, ensuring a tight seal around each agnolotto. After pinching, use a pasta cutter or knife to trim along the sealed edges, separating the dough into small, individual agnolotti. Repeat with the remaining pasta sheets and filling.

5. Bring a large pot of salted water to a boil over high heat. Drop half of the agnolotti into the boiling water and stir gently. Cook until they float to the surface, about 1 minute. Scoop out the agnolotti with a slotted spoon. Repeat with the second half of the agnolotti. Reserve 1 cup / 250 ml of the pasta water.

6. Meanwhile, heat a large saucepan over medium-high heat and add half of the reserved braising liquid and 1½ tablespoons of the butter. Bring to a simmer. Add half of the cooked agnolotti to the saucepan and a bit of the pasta water if the sauce is too dry. Repeat with the second batch. Serve immediately.

Ravioli Pasta Dough

Serves 4 to 6 (150 to 160 ravioli)

1⅔ cups / 200 g tipo "00" or all-purpose flour

2 large eggs, at room temperature

2 large egg yolks, at room temperature

Rice flour, for dusting (see Note)

1. Mound the tipo "00" flour on a work surface. Make a well in the center of the flour and add the eggs and egg yolks. Using a fork, beat the eggs gently together. Slowly incorporate the flour, starting with the inner sides of the well.

2. When the dough begins to come together, start kneading using just your palms with a back-and-forth motion (the joke is that you should always be able to answer the phone while making pasta!). Use a dough scraper to scrape away any stray bits around the pasta dough, as dried-out dough will interfere with your pasta making and make it lumpy. The dough is ready when it is elastic and the surface gently "comes back to you" when pressed, 15 to 30 minutes.

3. Place the dough in a large bowl and cover with a lid, a cotton cloth, or a plate. Set aside in the coolest part of your kitchen for 1 hour. (You can also prepare the dough the day before, wrap it in plastic wrap, and refrigerate. Before rolling, bring it back to room temperature.)

4. When ready to roll out the dough, dust a work surface and rolling pin lightly with rice flour. Cut off a piece of dough (the equivalent of a handful), press with your palm onto the work surface, and roll out with the rolling pin to about ½ inch / 1.25 cm thick. Set a pasta machine to its thickest setting and roll the pasta dough through it.

5. Switch the pasta machine to the next thinnest setting and roll the pasta dough through again. Continue switching the settings lower and lower until you get a thin and perfectly smooth sheet of pasta, about dial 7. Repeat with the remaining dough.

6. Place the pasta sheet on the floured work surface. Cut and/or stuff the pasta according to your liking. The pasta will be fine at room temperature for up to 30 minutes, but if you're cooking later, cover the pasta with plastic wrap and refrigerate for up to 24 hours. You can also freeze individual portions for up to 3 months, making sure they are well wrapped.

NOTE

Why rice flour?

It's a light, gluten-free flour that's silky smooth; it won't thicken the water when you cook the pasta and will prevent sticking.

BRACIOLE NAPOLETANE

Neapolitan Meat Rolls in Tomato Sauce with Pasta

Involtini in Italian simply means "rolls." Various types of involtini are common in the South: In Sicily they are fond of involtini di spada (swordfish rolls), and in Naples they love these meat rolls, often called braciole. Neapolitan ragù is made by cooking a large piece of veal or beef in tomato sauce, then the fork-tender meat is loosely broken up and served with a pasta. This is a variation on the ragù napoletano, an even better version in my opinion, in which the large piece of meat is the involtini that's cooked gently in the sauce, each lending the other its wonderful flavors.

Most often, involtini are served on their own, with side dishes like potatoes and sautéed greens. In our house, we tend to make them with extra sauce so we can use some of it for pasta. My husband, a purist, likes to eat the pasta first, then the meat and vegetables. Here I like to skip the potatoes and serve it all together as one complete dish. We will never agree on this.

6 slices beef, top round or flank steak or sirloin (1 pound / 500 g total)

A generous handful of fresh parsley, finely chopped

Fine sea salt and freshly ground black pepper

6 slices pancetta

2 garlic cloves, thinly sliced

3 tablespoons extra-virgin olive oil

1 cup / 250 ml dry white wine

Two 28-ounce / 800 g cans peeled tomatoes, chopped

1 pound / 500 g dried penne, rigatoni, or bucatini

SERVES 4 TO 6

1. Pat the beef dry, then cover with a sheet of plastic wrap and pound each slice with a meat pounder to ¼ inch / 6 mm thick.

2. Sprinkle the beef with the parsley and season with salt and pepper. Place a slice of pancetta on top of each piece of beef and top with a slice of garlic. Roll up each slice and secure each with a toothpick.

3. In a Dutch oven, heat the olive oil over medium heat. Add the rolls and cook until browned on all sides, 3 minutes, then add the wine.

4. Once the wine has cooked off, add the tomatoes. Reduce the heat to low. Cover and cook, turning the rolls occasionally, until the rolls are fork-tender, about 2 hours. Discard the toothpicks. Taste the sauce and season with salt and pepper.

5. Bring a large pot of salted water to a boil over high heat. Add the pasta and cook to al dente according to the package directions, then drain. Set aside the beef rolls on a plate. Add the pasta to the sauce in the pot and toss so it is well coated. Serve immediately with the beef rolls.

BAKED TAGLIOLINI *with* PROSCIUTTO

Harry's Bar in Venice is one of my favorite places on earth. It's an institution and home to many legends. My rule of thumb when I go there is never to order anything inventive, just the classics: the carpaccio, some other staples, and definitely this baked pasta. It is such a simple dish, almost childishly comforting and, at the same time, luxurious. In the same way that a fresh baguette with butter, dipped in a perfectly soft-boiled egg, can be luxurious, baked tagliolini is a triumph of uncomplicated cooking, in which béchamel, one of the cornerstones of French cooking, merges with Italian tagliolini and prosciutto. Of course the kids love this dish (kids of any age do), but they rarely get to go to Harry's Bar, so they asked me to make it at home. I was hesitant—could I re-create the magic? Turns out I could, and so can you.

4 tablespoons / 60 g unsalted butter

4 ounces / 115 g prosciutto, very thinly sliced crosswise

12 ounces / 350 g dried tagliolini

1½ cups / 150 g grated Parmigiano Reggiano cheese

Fine sea salt and freshly ground black pepper

1 cup / 250 ml Béchamel (page 98)

SERVES 4

1. Bring a large pot of salted water to a boil over high heat.

2. Meanwhile, in a large skillet, melt 1 tablespoon / 15 g of the butter over medium-high heat. Add the prosciutto and cook, stirring constantly, until lightly browned and fragrant, 1 to 2 minutes.

3. Add the pasta to the boiling water and cook to al dente according to the package directions. Drain the pasta, then add it to the skillet with the prosciutto and toss to combine. Add another 2 tablespoons / 30 g of the butter and toss until melted. Sprinkle half of the Parmigiano Reggiano over the pasta and toss again to combine. Season with salt and pepper.

4. Transfer the pasta to an 8-inch / 20 cm square baking dish and spread it out evenly. Spoon the béchamel over the pasta, then sprinkle with the remaining Parmigiano Reggiano. Cut the remaining tablespoon of butter into small pieces and scatter over the cheese.

5. Preheat the broiler. Place the baking dish 4 to 6 inches / 10 to 15 cm under the broiler and broil until browned and bubbling, 1 to 2 minutes. Let cool slightly and serve.

LASAGNA NAPOLITANA *with* MEATBALLS

Ragù

2 tablespoons extra-virgin olive oil

1 large onion, chopped

14 ounces / 400 g ground pork

½ cup / 120 ml dry white wine

2 cups / 500 ml tomato passata

Fine sea salt

Meatballs

4 ounces / 120 g stale bread, torn into small pieces

⅓ cup / 70 ml whole milk

10 ounces / 300 g ground pork, veal, or beef

1 large egg

1 tablespoon dried breadcrumbs

½ teaspoon ground nutmeg

3 tablespoons grated Parmigiano Reggiano cheese

1 teaspoon fine sea salt and 1 teaspoon freshly ground black pepper

Extra-virgin olive oil, for frying

Assembly

15 ounces / 425 g ricotta cheese, drained

8 ounces / 250 g fresh lasagna sheets

5 ounces / 150 g fresh mozzarella cheese, chopped into small pieces (make sure to pat the mozzarella dry to avoid excess water)

5 ounces / 150 g provola, provolone, or scamorza cheese, coarsely grated

3½ ounces / 100 g grated Parmigiano Reggiano cheese

2 hard-boiled eggs, peeled and sliced

SERVES 4

Lasagna is often a slightly misunderstood dish. Not that it really matters because most versions are terribly satisfying, and the result is always more important than how it's "supposed" to be done. Still, culinary heritage is important if only in the spirit of knowing the traditions before breaking them.

The most famous lasagna is likely the Bolognese version, at least in name, which uses a ragù that includes fewer tomatoes. You can get good lasagna all over Italy and outside of Bologna. In the South, you can really feel the tomatoes. This tells only some of the story of a real Neapolitan lasagna, which, in addition to more tomatoes, has an impressive lineup of half the good food of Campania: eggs, various cheeses, tasty ragù, and . . . meatballs. I remember the first time I had it, I couldn't believe the joyful richness of this dish. You could say this is what happens when you merge a lasagna and a timpano. It's heaven.

1. **Make the ragù.** Heat the olive oil in a medium saucepan over medium heat. Add the onion and sauté until golden, about 4 minutes.

2. Add the pork and cook, breaking it up occasionally, until browned, 8 minutes. Add the wine and cook until evaporated, 2 minutes more. Reduce the heat to medium-low. Add the tomato passata and 1 cup / 250 ml water and season with salt. Cook until you have a smooth and rich sauce, about 1 hour. Set aside.

3. **Meanwhile, make the meatballs.** In a small bowl, combine the bread and milk. Set aside and let the bread completely absorb the milk. Squeeze out the excess milk and place the bread in a large bowl. Add the pork, egg, breadcrumbs, nutmeg, Parmigiano Reggiano, salt, and pepper and mix to combine evenly. Shape into meatballs about 1 inch / 2.5 cm in diameter.

4. Line a plate with paper towels. Pour 1 inch / 2.5 cm olive oil into a large, high-sided pan. Heat the oil to about 375°F / 190°C over medium heat. You can test whether the oil is ready by dropping in a small piece of bread. If the bread turns golden brown immediately, the oil is ready. Working in batches, brown the meatballs on all sides, 5 to 6 minutes. Transfer to the paper towel–lined plate to drain.

5. Preheat the oven to 350°F / 180°C.

6. **Assemble the lasagna.** In a medium bowl, gently combine the ricotta with 2 ladlefuls of the ragù.

7. Add one-third of the ragù to the bottom of a 9 × 13-inch / 23 × 33 cm baking dish in an even layer. Top with a single layer of lasagna sheets. Spread one-third of the ricotta mixture over the lasagna sheets in an even layer. Top with one-third of the meatballs and sprinkle with about one-third of the mozzarella and provola.

8. Repeat the process twice, adding the egg and Parmigiano to the middle layer along with the mozzarella and provola. Bake until golden and bubbling, about 30 minutes. Let cool for 10 minutes before serving.

60

TAGLIOLINI *with* WHITE TRUFFLES & BUTTER

Whenever we are traveling in Italy and tell any Italian that we live in Turin, they will almost always mention three things. Barolo and the white truffles of Alba (both approvingly, "Mamma mia, che buono"), and Juventus, the local football club (less approvingly, hated by Neapolitans, "Juve e la Marda"). The reputation of the white truffles has traveled well beyond the shores of Italy. They have acquired a mythical status in the culinary world and are considered (even by many French) as superior even to the black truffles of Périgord. Foreigners flock to the Langhe (the province where Alba is located), an hour south of Turin, from late October until Christmas in search of truffled bliss.

All this acclaim has seen prices rise steadily, but luckily we have a greengrocer in Torino who knows where to get them and when. He refuses to budge on the price, and he never fails. When he's happy with the quality and the price, so am I.

We love to serve the first white truffles each year by simply grating them on large fried farm eggs or using them in an egg cocotte. Whatever is left the following day we use to perfume scrambled eggs for breakfast. Serving white truffles with the local tagliolini (usually made with an abundance of egg yolks) is how the Piemontese most commonly enjoy their yearly truffles. It may be the most luxurious and simple pasta dish on earth. Note: *Tajarin* is *tagliolini* in the Piemontese dialect.

14 ounces / 400 g fresh tagliolini (recipe follows)

1½ ounces / 40 g white truffle (see Note)

5 tablespoons / 70 g unsalted butter

2 ounces / 60 g Parmigiano Reggiano cheese, grated (optional)

Fine sea salt and freshly ground black pepper

SERVES 4

1. Bring a large pot of salted water to a boil over high heat. Add the pasta and cook until al dente, 1 minute. Reserving 1 cup / 250 ml pasta water, drain the pasta.

2. Meanwhile, wipe the truffle with a damp cloth to remove any dirt. Grate half of the truffle.

3. In a large skillet, melt the butter over medium-low heat until it foams. Reduce the heat to low. Add the grated truffle along with the reserved pasta cooking water. Add the drained pasta to the pan along with the Parmigiano Reggiano, if using. Toss until well coated. Season with salt and pepper.

4. Shave the remaining truffle over the pasta and serve immediately.

NOTE

You will need a truffle shaver for this recipe. Alternatively, a good mandoline can do the trick.

recipe continues »

Fresh Tagliolini or Tajarin

Makes 14 ounces / 400 g pasta

1⅔ cups / 200 g tipo "00" or all-purpose flour

6 large egg yolks

1 tablespoon dry white wine

Rice flour, for dusting (see Note on page 169)

1. Mound the tipo "00" flour on a work surface. Make a well in the center of the flour and add the egg yolks. Using a fork, beat the egg yolks gently together with the wine. Slowly incorporate the flour, starting with the inner sides of the well.

2. When the dough begins to come together, start kneading using just your palms with a back-and-forth motion (the joke is that you should always be able to answer the phone while making pasta!). Use a dough scraper to scrape away any stray bits around the pasta dough, as dried-out dough will interfere with your pasta and make it lumpy. The dough is ready when it is elastic and the surface gently "comes back to you" when pressed, 15 to 30 minutes.

3. Place the dough in a large bowl and cover with a lid, a cotton cloth, or a plate. Set aside in the coolest part of your kitchen for 1 hour. (You can also prepare the dough the day before, wrap it in plastic wrap, and refrigerate. Before rolling, bring it back to room temperature.)

4. When ready to roll out the dough, dust a work surface and rolling pin lightly with rice flour. Cut off a piece of dough (the equivalent of a handful), press with your palm onto the work surface, and roll out with the rolling pin to about ½ inch / 1.25 cm thick. Set a pasta machine to its thickest setting and roll the pasta dough through it.

5. Switch the pasta machine to the next thinnest setting and roll the pasta dough through again. Continue switching the settings lower and lower until you get a thin and perfectly smooth sheet of pasta (about dial 7). Repeat with the remaining dough.

6. Place the pasta sheets on the floured work surface. Fold the sheets upon themselves loosely. Using a sharp knife, cut the folded sheets into very thin strands—about ⅛ inch / 3 mm thick. Fluff up the strands to untangle them and place them in small nests on a wooden board dusted with rice flour.

RISOTTO TORCELLANA

The ratio of pasta dinners to risotto dinners in our kitchen is probably ten to one in favor of pasta. Risotto takes a bit longer to make, and there are so many good pasta options that sometimes we simply forget about our friend the risotto. But not for long because when we want a risotto, we really want it, so much it almost becomes an obsession. Often risotto-making in our house is linked with something very seasonal. Asparagus risotto in the spring is on everyone's list of favorites. So is risotto with porcini in the fall.

I had a version of this risotto for the first time at Locanda Cipriani on Torcello in the Venetian lagoon. It's a wonderful establishment founded by Harry's Bar proprietor, Giuseppe Cipriani. His good friend Ernest Hemingway stayed there when he wanted to get away from his drinking buddies in Venice. Essentially, this is a vegetable risotto that uses some of the more common vegetables like carrot, zucchini, and eggplant with the addition of other more seasonal ingredients when they are available. I like it best when porcinis are in season, as they lend this dish an autumnal feel, but you can substitute simple mushrooms.

1 quart / liter vegetable stock

6 tablespoons / 90 ml extra-virgin olive oil, plus more for drizzling

1 medium eggplant, cut into small dice

1 red bell pepper

1 small leek, thinly sliced

1 small onion, finely chopped

2 zucchinis, finely chopped

1 ounce / 30 g white mushrooms, thinly sliced

1 ounce / 30 g fresh porcini mushrooms, cleaned and chopped

Fine sea salt and freshly ground black pepper

1½ cups / 300 g carnaroli rice

1 shallot, diced

1 ounce / 30 g artichoke hearts, thinly sliced (optional)

2 tablespoons / 30 g unsalted butter

2 tablespoons grated Parmigiano Reggiano cheese

SERVES 4

1. In a large saucepan, bring the stock to a simmer over medium-high heat. Reduce the heat to low to keep the stock at a simmer.

2. In a large sauté pan, heat 2 tablespoons of the olive oil over medium heat. Add the eggplant and sauté until tender, about 3 minutes. Transfer to a plate and let cool. Reserve the pan.

3. Roast the pepper directly over a gas flame or under the broiler, turning occasionally, until charred all over, 5 to 7 minutes. When cool enough to handle, peel and seed the pepper, then cut into small dice.

4. In the previously reserved sauté pan, heat another 2 tablespoons of olive oil over medium heat. Add the leek and onion and cook until browned, about 2 minutes. Increase the heat to high. Add the zucchini and cook until golden, 2 minutes. Add the mushrooms, roasted pepper, and eggplant and cook until browned and crispy, about 10 minutes total. Season with salt and pepper. Transfer to a plate.

5. In the same pan, heat the remaining 2 tablespoons olive oil over medium heat. Add the rice and shallot and cook until the rice is toasted, 2 minutes. Add a ladle of the hot stock and gently stir. When the liquid is mostly absorbed, add another ladle of stock, stirring constantly and adding more to keep the rice covered at all times. Repeat this process until the rice is creamy but still al dente, 15 to 20 minutes. Stir in the artichoke hearts, if using, and cooked vegetables, reserving a spoonful for serving, and cook until the flavors meld, about 1 minute.

6. Add the butter, a drizzle of olive oil, the Parmigiano Reggiano, and a pinch of salt and pepper to taste, stirring vigorously to make the risotto creamier. Serve immediately topped with the reserved vegetables.

A World of Interiors

Our friends Paulo and Costantino have a beautiful apartment in Milan. They are architects, blessed with good taste and two spare bedrooms, and when we're in town, they often invite us to stay the night. We love spending time at their place, and I'm always sad to leave. There is something so nice about their apartment. It's tastefully decorated and very livable. They are collectors, and while the rooms are not exactly minimalist, nothing feels cluttered either. I always feel their apartment is much more put together than ours. My husband agrees; he blames it on me.

Inside one of Paulo's well-arranged cabinets, one that stores linens or towels, there is an old French sign that says, "Une place pour chaque chose et chaque chose à sa place," which translates, more or less, into: "A place for everything and everything in its place." Oddur tried to buy the sign from Paulo—he wanted to hang it in one of my closets—but Paulo wouldn't part with it. I do agree with the principle, but it's hard for me to practice it. When a space opens up in any cabinet or closet, someone else will put something else in its place. I admit that we're quite bad in our family. You might find the toaster where the printer is usually stored. Or I take out the big pasta pot and a vacancy is created, then it might be filled with absolutely anything. The kids think tidying their room means putting everything under the bed. I'm exaggerating a little bit, but only a little. My husband's closet looks like a men's store or a scene from *American Psycho.* Mine, it's a cabinet of curiosities, a Pandora's box. I discover new things in there all the time; it's beautiful.

Our version of the French proverb is "Everything has a place, somewhere."

When making a home, the first thing to achieve, I believe, is that those who live there are happy and relaxed and enjoy being there. A home is not a museum or an installation. It should be livable first. Then beautiful. We strive for both.

Livable means comfortable and functional and safe. I prize a big, hot bathtub, plenty of space for my toiletries, a large, luxurious bed with soft bed linens and pillows, like a great hotel. We have already discussed the kitchen, so let's talk about the dining room. Some meals are meant for the kitchen, but it's so nice to have a slightly more formal room where we use the fancy china and the good silver. We always dine by candlelight, and I really don't like bright overhead lighting. Plenty of lamps in corners is how I like it; they create a cozy and inviting mood.

My husband is a minimalist at heart. He likes masculine, well-made stuff, typically from the '30s to the '60s. He puts beauty above comfort. I like flowery prints and sofas you can sink into and silk drapes and rugs on the floor. I could see myself living in a Venetian palazzo. I could see my husband sitting in a convent-like room with one candle.

A marriage is about finding a balance, how to live and be happy. Part of that is building a space where we both feel at home. I think we've come up with a few guidelines that work for us. I know which rooms are most important to me, and I claim sovereignty over those. The bathroom is mine; so is the bedroom. And the room next to the bedroom. I also claim the children's rooms. Somehow we both agree completely on the kitchen, which is a relief. I also let Oddur take the early rounds in many of the common spaces; he has good taste, after all, so I have nothing to worry about. But his perfectly curated chambers will soon enough be peppered with cute little finds, the windows covered with drapes, a lamp here (I love lamps), a pillow or a blanket there. When we travel and pass by antique stores, Oddur tries to divert me. When he sees me pick up a lamp at a flea market, he starts to shiver and sweat. I sometimes buy mismatching plates and hide them in the laundry or in a sock drawer. In some ways you could say that I love objects more than spaces. I like souvenirs from travels and mementos from the past. If I receive a thoughtful gift, even if it's not to my taste, I feel compelled to put it somewhere, but Oddur is utterly ruthless in those types of situations, which I must admit can be expedient.

The lady who lived in our current apartment before us had been there for a long time. She had seen her husband die and her children grow up, and then she continued living there, alone, in that huge apartment for many years. She loved the apartment and collecting things, so she ended up having more objects in every room than most people have in entire houses. She must think the apartment looks terribly empty now, but she has nothing to worry about; I'll fill it up slowly, and while I don't really want to match her for quantity, she won't be disappointed in my additions. My husband will watch it unfold as the years go by. From an uncomfortable chair.

PORCINI FRITTI

When we lived in the French countryside, we used to pick our own porcini (or cèpes, as they are known in France) as a family sport. We had them raw, in omelets, or sautéed as a side dish. We don't hunt for them in the forest these days, but as soon as the conditions are right, we head for the markets and pursue them there. Northern Italy has rich porcini traditions, and you can find them in abundance as early as summer and culminating in the fall when it gets too cold.

Here in Italy, they are very fond of deep-frying anything they can, and porcinis are no exception. There is nothing better than going to your local trattoria and, upon entering, seeing a stack of the freshest porcini ready to be cooked. Sometimes we order a bunch of fried ones for the table while we peruse the menu, but fried porcini are equally delightful as a side dish with a good piece of meat or fish. At home I like to make them when it's just me and my husband (even with so many kids, it does happen, albeit rarely). A mountain of freshly fried porcini and a really good bottle of wine for two.

1 cup / 120 g all-purpose flour

2 cups / 200 g dried breadcrumbs

2 large eggs

1 pound / 500 g fresh porcini mushrooms, cut into 1-inch / 2.5 cm thick slices

Vegetable oil, for frying

Fine sea salt and freshly ground black pepper

SERVES 6

1. Place the flour in a shallow bowl and the breadcrumbs in another. In a third shallow bowl, beat the eggs. One at a time, dredge the mushrooms in the flour, then dip into the egg. Let any excess drip off, then coat in the breadcrumbs. Transfer to a parchment paper–lined plate.

2. Line a large plate with paper towels. Pour 1 inch / 2.5 cm oil into a large, high-sided pan. Heat the oil to about 350°F / 180°C over medium-high heat. You can test whether the oil is hot enough by adding in a small drop of batter. If it sizzles and turns golden and crisp, the oil is ready. Working in batches, add the mushrooms to the oil and fry until crispy and golden, about 1 minute per side. Transfer to the paper towel–lined plate to drain.

3. Season with salt and pepper and serve immediately.

POLLO ALLA CACCIATORA

Hunter's Chicken

Hunter's chicken is a very popular family dish in Italy, made all over the country but stemming originally from the heartlands of Tuscany. The principles of dishes like this are mostly similar: White meats like chicken or rabbit are braised in wine with onions, herbs, and often tomatoes or peppers. Each family makes a different version, which is endearing, but in our family, we have two different approaches within the same household, which is more complicated and can lead to conflict. My husband loves all things tomato, and he favors a heavy dose of canned tomatoes and prefers to use red wine. I like to make a version that's more "in bianco," although I don't mind including a few tomatoes.

Without ever having specific negotiations to reach an official cacciatora treaty, the laws of harmonious marriage have led us to this version. It's probably closer to my taste than his, which is simply the privilege of the cook who most often makes this dish.

6 chicken breasts and/or thighs and drumsticks

Fine sea salt and freshly ground black pepper

1 teaspoon all-purpose flour, plus more for dredging

4 tablespoons / 60 ml extra-virgin olive oil

1 medium onion, chopped

2 celery ribs, chopped

1 medium carrot, chopped

8 ounces / 250 g white mushrooms, chopped

1 garlic clove, minced

1 teaspoon chopped fresh thyme

1 teaspoon chopped fresh rosemary

21 ounces / 600 g canned peeled tomatoes, diced

½ cup / 120 ml dry white wine

1 cup / 250 ml vegetable or chicken stock

SERVES 4 TO 6

1. Pat the chicken dry and season with salt. Place flour in a shallow bowl and dredge the chicken in the flour. Shake off the excess.

2. In a large, heavy skillet, heat 2 tablespoons of the olive oil over medium heat. Working in batches, add the chicken and cook, turning once, until golden brown on both sides, about 15 minutes. Transfer to a plate, then discard the oil. Wipe out the pan.

3. Add the remaining 2 tablespoons oil to the skillet and heat over medium heat. Add the onion, celery, carrot, mushrooms, and garlic and cook until tender, about 10 minutes. Stir in the thyme, rosemary, and tomatoes and increase the heat to high. Add the wine and bring to a boil. Cook for 3 to 4 minutes, then reduce the heat to medium. Stir in the 1 teaspoon flour and cook, stirring, until thickened, 2 to 3 minutes.

4. Add the stock and cook, stirring, until well combined, 2 to 3 minutes more. Reduce the heat to low and simmer until the sauce has thickened, about 2 minutes. Return the chicken to the pan and spoon some of the vegetable mixture over the top. Bring to a simmer and cook, partially covered, until the chicken is cooked through and tender, about 15 minutes per side. Season to taste with salt and pepper. Serve immediately.

SCHOOL-NIGHT CHICKEN "MILANESE"

To my Italian friends who take food seriously—and believe me, many of them do—this dish is, well, not exactly a travesty but an absolute anomaly. Costoletta Milanese, or simply "Milanese," as it's known everywhere, is always made with breaded veal and only veal. To use other meats, especially a humble chicken, they say is fine (then they add, "for children"), but it's simply thought of as breaded chicken, not Milanese. A delightful friend of mine with great taste and an opinion on everything once took her husband to a restaurant in Sorrento. The menu listed one of the main dishes as "chicken Milanese," much to my friend's dismay. She swiftly summoned the headwaiter and proceeded to tell him that first, they were in Campania, so they should not offer quasi-international, or in any case northern Italian, dishes. And second, that no such thing as a chicken Milanese existed. Either way, it was a huge disappointment to her. The headwaiter had no words but decided, instead of doing nothing, to take their order. She ordered the caprese salad, while her husband, sheepishly, ordered the chicken Milanese.

Whatever the name, this is a universal crowd-pleaser among the young ones, and I must admit that I love it, too.

4 chicken breasts

½ teaspoon fine sea salt

¼ teaspoon freshly ground black pepper

1 cup / 120 g all-purpose flour

1½ cups / 150 g panko breadcrumbs

½ cup / 50 g grated Parmigiano Reggiano cheese

2 large eggs, beaten

1 cup / 250 ml extra-virgin olive oil, plus more as needed

SERVES 4

1. Slice each chicken breast horizontally into two thin cutlets. Cover the cutlets with a sheet of plastic wrap and pound each with a meat pounder to ½ inch / 1.25 cm thick. Season with the salt and pepper.

2. Place the flour in a shallow bowl. In a second shallow bowl, combine the panko and Parmigiano Reggiano. In a third shallow bowl, beat the eggs. Dredge the chicken in the flour, then dip into the eggs. Coat the chicken in the breadcrumb mixture and place on a plate.

3. Line a large plate with paper towels. In a large skillet over medium-high heat, heat the oil until sizzling. Working in batches, add the cutlets and fry until deep golden brown and cooked through, about 3 minutes per side. Transfer to the paper towel–lined plate to drain and repeat with the remaining cutlets, adding more oil as needed. Serve immediately.

COTOLETTA ALLA BOLOGNESE

When temperatures start falling, our appetite for, shall we say, more substantial dishes, tends to reappear. After all the tomato pastas and seafood of summer, we start longing for melted cheese, baked dishes, meat, and cream. A well-made Cotoletta alla Bolognese is one of the most delicious things in the heftier category of Italian dishes, but it's also dangerous. You should never make one per person, always share—remember that we are essentially looking at a dish on top of a dish, and every layer is filled with richness and goodness. The second thing to remember is not to make this recipe too early in the fall. I know, in the same way you are dying to swap your summer dresses and wear that handsome new tweed coat, you are fantasizing about a meal in front of the fireplace, heavy flavors, and big red wines. All I can say is, it will be cold soon enough, and like the tweeds, this dish can wait until November.

NOTE

You can choose a cutlet that is boneless or one with the bone in, although I find bone-in cutlets tastier.

1. Cover the cutlets with a sheet of plastic wrap and pound each with a meat pounder to ½ inch / 1.25 mm thick.

2. In a medium bowl, beat the eggs with the Parmigiano Reggiano, nutmeg, salt, and pepper. Stir in the cream.

3. Place the breadcrumbs in a shallow bowl. Dip each veal slice in the egg mixture, then coat in the breadcrumbs, pressing to adhere, until well coated.

4. Line a plate with paper towels. Pour 1 inch / 2.5 cm oil into a large, high-sided pan. Heat the oil to about 350°F / 180°C over medium-high heat. You can test whether the oil is hot enough by adding in a small drop of batter. If it sizzles and turns golden and crisp, the oil is ready. Add the veal and fry until golden brown, 2 minutes on each side. Using tongs, transfer the veal to the paper towel–lined plate to drain and cool slightly.

5. Lay a slice of prosciutto over the top of each veal cutlet, covering it completely.

6. Sprinkle with Parmigiano Reggiano, ensuring it's evenly distributed over the ham.

7. In a medium skillet, heat the stock over medium-high heat until it begins to simmer. Add the veal cutlets, ham and cheese side facing up. Bring the stock to a boil, then reduce the heat to a gentle simmer.

8. Cover the skillet and cook until the cheese has melted and the veal is cooked through, about 3 minutes. Transfer the veal cutlets to serving plates.

9. Drizzle a little of the simmered stock over the top of the veal before serving.

4 veal cutlets, about 8 ounces / 250 g each

4 large eggs

1 cup / 100 g grated Parmigiano Reggiano cheese, plus more for sprinkling

Pinch of ground nutmeg

1 teaspoon fine sea salt

1 teaspoon freshly ground black pepper

¼ cup / 60 ml heavy cream

1 cup / 100 g dried breadcrumbs

Extra-virgin olive oil, for frying

4 slices prosciutto

1 cup / 240 ml vegetable stock

SERVES 4 TO 6

FILETTO AL PEPE VERDE

Filet Mignon with Brandy Cream Sauce & Green Peppercorns

This recipe is heavily influenced by French cuisine, or even more than that, it's simply French food cooked in Italy. Italians rarely use sauces on their meat (unless the meat is braised in the sauce), and most steaks in Italy are served on their own, such as the famous bistecca fiorentina, which needs no other companions than oil, salt, and the Sangiovese in your glass. French cuisine, on the other hand, revolves around sauces. You won't find this way of serving beef all over Italy but in Piemonte, which was originally a French settlement and ruled for centuries by the Savoy family of France (they were the first kings of a united Italy). My only "beef" with this recipe is that, since I grew up on French beef, which is fattier than the leaner Fassona cows of Piemonte, it usually takes me a while to find a piece I'm happy with—though the Fassona beef is certainly excellent in braised dishes and the famous carne cruda, or raw meat, preparations of the region.

Four 8-ounce / 250 g filet mignon steaks

Fine sea salt

1 tablespoon all-purpose flour

4 tablespoons / 60 g clarified butter

3 tablespoons brandy

1 cup / 250 ml beef or chicken stock

⅔ cup / 160 ml heavy cream

2 tablespoons Dijon mustard

¼ cup / 36 g whole green peppercorns

SERVES 4

1. Preheat the oven to 350°F / 180°C.

2. Sprinkle the steaks generously with salt. Place the flour on a plate and dredge the steaks very lightly.

3. In a large sauté pan, melt the clarified butter over high heat. When the pan is sizzling hot, add the steaks and sear on one side, without moving, until golden brown, 4 minutes. Flip gently and cook on the other side for 1 minute. Transfer to an ovenproof dish and place in the preheated oven for 3 to 5 minutes, depending on the type of doneness you desire.

4. Over medium heat, pour in the brandy, then tilt the pan away from you and carefully ignite the alcohol to flambé. Once the flames subside, reduce the heat to low and add the stock, cream, mustard, and peppercorns. Bring the mixture to a gentle boil, allowing it to reduce until thick and glossy, about 2 minutes.

5. Transfer the steaks to a serving plate and spoon the sauce all over. Serve immediately.

DRAPPIER
CHAMPAGNE
DRAPPIER
Carte d'Or

How to Set a Table

I'm at once very frivolous about table settings and very formal. Let me explain what I mean. By formal, I mean that the table has to be laid out beautifully. Good-looking, heavy plates, silverware (although god knows ours could be polished more regularly). Beautiful, appropriate glasses for the wine being served that night and simple ones for water. There are rules, of course, on how to set the cutlery and the glasses, how to align them and fold the napkins. That's all very good, but I'm not a stickler for any of that. My table has to be beautiful, warm, and inviting. Stylish but never too stiff—that's rule number one.

Candles are an absolute must. So that's rule number two. A few are enough but more are better. And flowers. When I have big tables and lots of space, I like to decorate with fresh fruits and vegetables. Ideally what's freshest and in season, like cherries that our guests can just reach out for at will during the meal. In the middle of the table, I like to put an "orto," a little vegetable garden. This might be one large vase that holds herbs and flowers, a bit wild, that represents nature. I like to combine the herbs I use for cooking with a bit of color from the flowers. Paper napkins are outlawed; we like vintage cloth napkins we have collected over the years in various places, heavy linen or cotton that's a delight to touch. (And never get attached to your napkins. They won't all survive; that's their job.) I don't like an overhead light; lamps in corners are better, and plants that cast shadows on the walls. The music should fit the mood. Chet Baker or Billie Holiday always works wonders.

In the end it all comes down to "sprezzatura," the art of making things look effortless, even if they perhaps weren't. The word is most often used in the context of dressing, but I think it can apply to anything, from cooking to setting the table to how you decorate your apartment. Nothing should feel laborious; it makes your guests uncomfortable and does little for the mood. The table may look lovely, but nobody suffered; it just happened somehow.

APPLE RICOTTA CAKE

If you divide desserts into categories, then some would be called decadent, others luxurious, festive, or fit for a wedding. Some are distinctively "granny." The last category is home to all the heartening, unfussy, and everyday (in a perfect world) treats that the best Italian nonna would make for her grandchildren when they come home from school, tired and slightly disillusioned because the novel thrill of back to school has worn out and all that awaits them are early mornings, math tests, and essays. Sometimes when I'm working at home and start thinking about my little ones, imagining them sitting in their classrooms looking at the clock, I make this cake out of love for them. I am the mommy, but sometimes I'm the granny, too.

7 ounces / 200 g ricotta cheese

2 large eggs

1¾ cups / 210 g all-purpose flour, sifted

½ cup / 50 g almond flour

¼ cup / 50 g granulated sugar

1 tablespoon baking powder

½ teaspoon fine sea salt

⅔ cup / 150 ml whole milk

Grated zest and juice of ½ lemon

7 tablespoons / 100 g unsalted butter, melted, plus more for greasing the pan

3 medium apples, peeled, cored, and diced (about 2½ cups)

4 teaspoons slivered almonds

SERVES 4

1. Preheat the oven to 350°F / 180°C. Grease a 9-inch / 23 cm cake pan with butter.

2. In a large bowl, using a fork, beat the ricotta with the eggs, adding one at a time. Mix in the flour, almond flour, sugar, baking powder, and salt. Gradually pour in the milk, stirring constantly, until the batter is smooth. Add the lemon zest and juice and melted butter and stir until incorporated. Gently fold the apples into the batter.

3. Pour the batter into the prepared cake pan. Sprinkle the almonds over the top.

4. Bake until golden brown and a toothpick inserted into the center comes out clean, 45 to 50 minutes. Let cool and serve.

TIRAMISÙ

Let's face it, there is nothing I can tell you about tiramisù that you haven't already heard. We've all had countless versions in various restaurants, usually good or pretty good. When I wrote my first Italian cookbook, *Old World Italian*, four years ago, I meant to include this recipe, but when we needed to edit out a few, the tiramisù didn't make the cut. I guess I felt it was almost banal to include such a well-known recipe, sort of like including a recipe for avocado toast. Delicious, yes, but really necessary? Let's say that in my case, the tiramisù became the victim of its own success. This time my flow of thinking is more along the lines of: This is a really classic, simple version. It will make anyone happy. And do I really want to make a second Italian cookbook and still not include a tiramisù? It would feel like an oversight. Finally, and most poetically, what if someone buys this book who's never ever heard of tiramisù? Imagine how happy they will be.

½ cup / 100 g granulated sugar
2 cups / 500 ml heavy cream
5 large egg yolks
2 large eggs
18 ounces / 500 g mascarpone
2 cups / 480 ml strong coffee
48 ladyfinger biscuits
Unsweetened cocoa, for dusting

SERVES 6

1. In a small saucepan, combine the sugar with 2 tablespoons water. Bring to a boil over medium heat. Cook until a syrup forms, about 5 minutes. Let it cool completely.

2. In a large bowl, use a hand mixer with a whisk attachment to whip the cream until stiff peaks form. In a separate large bowl, whisk the egg yolks and eggs until smooth. Whisk in the cooled sugar syrup. Fold in the mascarpone with a rubber spatula, then gently fold in the whipped cream until incorporated.

3. Pour the coffee into a medium bowl. Set out 6 serving plates. Working one at a time, dip the ladyfingers into the coffee, then transfer to a serving plate. Repeat this process until each serving plate has 4 soaked ladyfingers. Divide half the cream among the serving plates spreading it into an even layer over the soaked ladyfingers. Repeat with the remaining ladyfingers and cream.

4. Sprinkle the tiramisù with cocoa. Chill in the refrigerator until set, at least 2 hours, then serve.

MILLEFOGLIE

It's a wonderful piece of salesmanship calling a dessert that consists of no more than a few layers of puff pastry and pastry cream, a thousand layers. *Millefoglie* is the Italian translation of *millefeuille* in French, which means "a thousand sheets," and like many other recipes here in Piemonte, it is directly derived from France. My son Hudson, who, as it happens, recently started culinary school in Paris, is in love with millefoglie, and so was my father, who studied in Paris (I believe that food cravings can be inherited). Ceccarelli, an old-fashioned family restaurant in Turin where we often have lunches on Sunday, displays their desserts in the entrance, and Hudson always checked to see whether they had made a millefoglie. Usually they hadn't, but he always asked for it. After a few years, they just started making it for us, and the name Thorisson in the reservation book came to mean "Table for 7 + Millefoglie."

25 ounces / 700 g ricotta cheese

1⅔ cups / 200 g powdered sugar, sifted, plus more for dusting

Grated zest of 1 lemon

¾ cup plus 2 tablespoons / 200 ml heavy cream

Two 8-ounce / 250 g rolls refrigerated puff pastry (8 × 12 inches / 20 × 30 cm)

SERVES 6

NOTE

You can add chocolate chips or chopped summer berries to the cream layers, too.

1. In a large bowl, combine the ricotta, 1¼ cups / 125 g of the powdered sugar, and the lemon zest until smooth.

2. In a separate large bowl, use a hand mixer with a whisk attachment to whip the cream until stiff peaks form. Gently fold the whipped cream into the ricotta mixture until well combined. Cover and chill in the refrigerator to firm up.

3. Preheat the oven to 350°F / 180°C. Line a baking sheet with parchment paper.

4. Roll out a piece of puff pastry on top of the parchment paper. Carefully cut the pastry in half vertically so you get two sheets. Prick the pastry all over gently with a fork. Dust generously with half of the remaining powdered sugar. Transfer to a large baking sheet. Repeat with the remaining piece of puff pastry.

5. Bake until golden brown and puffed up, 12 to 15 minutes, rotating the baking sheets to ensure a uniform goldenness. Let cool on a wire rack.

6. Start by placing a large serving plate on your work surface. Spread a thin layer (about 1 tablespoon) of filling on the plate. This helps the first pastry sheet stay in place. Place the first pastry sheet on top of the prepared plate. Spread one-third of the ricotta filling evenly over the first pastry sheet, ensuring the filling reaches the edges. Place the second pastry sheet on top and spread another one-third of the ricotta filling evenly on top. Repeat the process with the third pastry sheet and the remaining ricotta filling. Top with the fourth pastry sheet and dust generously with powdered sugar. Transfer to the refrigerator and let set for at least 30 minutes before serving.

TORTA CAPRESE

While this cake hasn't conquered the world like the even more famous other caprese (the mozzarella and tomato salad), it has spread all over Italy and is among the nation's beloved desserts. While it is accepted that the Torta Caprese did indeed originate in Capri, the exact story remains disputed. One colorful version (and those often include royalty) suggests that the queen of Naples, who was of Austrian descent, requested a Sacher torte, but the bakers on Capri either did not know how to make it or didn't have the ingredients and mixed almonds in with the chocolate. As such, it falls into the category of happy mistakes, a long list of incidents where someone did something wrong, except it wasn't.

2 cups / 200 g almond flour

10 ounces / 300 g dark chocolate (70% cacao)

14 tablespoons / 200 g unsalted butter, plus extra for greasing

6 large eggs, separated

¾ cup plus 2 tablespoons / 180 g granulated sugar

Pinch of sea salt

1 tablespoon unsweetened cocoa powder

A squeeze of fresh lemon juice

Powdered sugar, for dusting

SERVES 10

1. Preheat the oven to 350°F / 180°C. Grease a 9-inch / 23 cm springform pan with butter and line the bottom with a round of parchment paper.

2. Heat a medium nonstick skillet over medium-low heat. Add the almond flour and toast until lightly browned, 2 minutes. Transfer to a plate and let cool.

3. Bring a medium pot of water to a boil over medium heat. Place a large, heatproof bowl on top of the pot. Add the chocolate and butter to the bowl and stir occasionally until melted and smooth, 8 to 10 minutes. Set aside to cool.

4. In a second large bowl, whisk together the egg yolks, granulated sugar, and salt until frothy and pale. Gradually pour the cooled, melted chocolate into the egg mixture, stirring constantly, until smooth and glossy. Gently fold in the cocoa powder and toasted almond flour until well combined.

5. In a third large bowl, whip the egg whites with a few drops of lemon juice with a hand mixer with a whisk attachment until stiff peaks form. Gently fold the whipped egg whites into the chocolate mixture, taking care not to deflate the batter.

6. Pour the batter into the prepared pan. Bake until a toothpick inserted into the center comes out clean, 20 to 25 minutes. Let the cake cool completely in the pan.

7. Before serving, dust with powdered sugar.

Inverno / Winter

Antipasti

Primi

Secondi

Dolci

CHRISTMAS EVE *with the* THORISSONS

GNOCCHI FRITTI *with* CULATELLO

In Emilia-Romagna, the home of Parma ham, mortadella, and culatello, they like to enjoy their salumi with bread. Gnocco fritto (also called torta fritta, depending on where you are in the region) is a type of simple, deep-fried bread that puffs up when it's fried.

Traditionally, gnocchi fritti are enjoyed with culatello, a type of high-quality cured ham, but they can also be served with other cured meats, cheeses, or as an accompaniment to a meal. Culatello is made in a relatively small appellation near Parma. It is considered the highest form of Italian salumi; only the best and leanest part of the pork thigh is used, while the rest goes into a traditional sausage.

If I was throwing a feast for the ages, a representation of the finest Italian cuisine has to offer, I would serve this unbeatable combo before anything else, with a glass of Italian sparkling wine.

6 tablespoons / 100 ml lukewarm water

½ teaspoon / 4 g active dry yeast

2 cups / 240 g all-purpose flour, plus more for dusting

1 tablespoon fine sea salt

2 tablespoons extra-virgin olive oil

Vegetable oil, for frying

24 slices culatello, for serving

MAKES 24 FRITTERS

NOTE

Traditionally, these are fried in lard for a rich taste.

1. Pour 2 tablespoons / 30 ml of the lukewarm water into a small bowl. Whisk in the yeast until dissolved. Let the yeast activate until frothy, 5 to 10 minutes.

2. Sift the flour into a large bowl. Make a well in the center and add the salt, olive oil, and activated yeast mixture and combine with a fork. Slowly incorporate the flour, starting with the inner sides of the well. Add the remaining lukewarm water, 1 tablespoon at a time, mixing after each addition to incorporate into the dough.

3. Transfer the dough to a lightly floured work surface. Knead it using your palms in a back-and-forth motion until the dough is elastic and slightly tacky, about 10 minutes. Roll the dough into a ball and transfer to a lightly oiled bowl. Cover the dough and let rise until doubled in size, about 1 hour.

4. Dust your work surface with more flour. Gently punch down the dough and turn it out. Roll out the dough with a rolling pin to about ⅛ inch / 3 mm thick. Using a sharp knife or pizza cutter, cut the dough into twenty-four 2- to 3-inch / 5 to 7.5 cm long diamonds.

5. Line a plate with paper towels. Pour 2 inches / 5 cm oil into a large, high-sided pan. Heat the oil to about 350°F / 180°C over medium heat. You can test whether the oil is hot enough by adding in a small drop of batter. If it sizzles and turns golden and crisp, the oil is ready. Working in batches, add the dough and cook until golden and puffed, 1 to 2 minutes per side. Transfer to the paper towel–lined plate to drain.

6. Arrange the culatello on a serving plate. Place the torta fritti on another plate and serve hot.

BAKED STUFFED ONIONS

Some Italian dishes have traveled the world, and others, it seems, have hardly left home. As I've said before, Piemontese cooking is much less known than that of neighboring regions. Panna cotta is the most famous export, followed perhaps by vitello tonnato—not to mention Nutella. If porcini and pumpkins signal the arrival of autumn, this is the dish that says "Now it's getting cold." It's a classic family dish from the wine country of Piemonte; you could even call it a peasant dish. At the same time, the stuffed onions feel strangely contemporary and elegant, like they had been conceived recently by an inventive chef on the prowl for accolades.

Whatever it feels like, this recipe is absolutely delicious, and I like to make it when I host dinner parties at home. Everyone gets their own onion, which is always a nice touch and easy to serve. Most people (outside of Piemonte) have never had it before, so it gets the guests talking. Most important, everyone loves it.

5 ounces / 150 g stale bread, cubed

½ cup / 120 ml whole milk

9 large yellow onions

Fine sea salt and freshly ground black pepper

10 ounces / 300 g Bra sausage or pork sausage, casings removed

A bunch of fresh parsley, finely chopped

1½ ounces / 50 g Toma di Rocaverano cheese, grated (or use a good melting cheese like Asiago)

1 tablespoon dried breadcrumbs

6 tablespoons / 90 ml extra-virgin olive oil

1 cup / 100 g grated Parmigiano Reggiano cheese

A few sprigs of fresh rosemary

SERVES 4 TO 6

1. Preheat the oven to 400°F / 200°C.

2. Place the bread in a large bowl. Toss with the milk and let sit until the milk is absorbed and the bread is soft, about 10 minutes.

3. Cut off the top ½ inch / 1.25 cm of each onion, then trim the bottom so that the onions will sit flat. Leave the onions in their peels. Using a spoon, scoop out the center of each onion, being careful not to pierce the bottom and leaving 2 to 3 outer layers intact. Season generously with salt and pepper. Finely chop the scooped-out onion interiors.

4. Using your hands, squeeze out any excess milk from the soaked bread and drain the milk. In the same bowl, add the sausage, parsley, Toma cheese, chopped onion, and breadcrumbs. Season with 1¼ teaspoons of salt and some pepper. Mix vigorously until well combined and smooth.

5. Place the onions hollow side up in a 9 × 13-inch / 23 × 33 cm baking dish. Stuff the sausage mixture into the onions, packing them tightly and mounding any extra filling on top. Drizzle with the olive oil and sprinkle with the Parmigiano Reggiano.

6. Place the sprigs of rosemary in the baking dish and pour in ½ cup / 120 ml water. Cover with foil and bake for 30 minutes. Remove the dish from the oven and remove the foil. Bake uncovered for another 10 to 15 minutes, until the onions are golden and the filling is bubbling. Alternatively, if entertaining, you can also do this in individual baking trays (see photo). Let the onions cool for 5 minutes before serving.

VENETIAN-STYLE DEEP-FRIED MEATBALLS

Cicchetti is a broad term used for all sorts of delicious bite-size (if you have a big mouth) plates that are enjoyed throughout the day and almost always accompanied by a glass of wine. Italians drink far less than those in neighboring countries, but Venetians are supposed to be the exception. This may be the reason. That and the rainy conditions.

Cicchetti are most often served as a piece of toasted bread with various toppings, but many other types of dishes qualify, such as these fried meatballs. Meatballs are often had as a second course here in Italy, after the pasta or rice, but in Venice they are very fond of snacking informally, much like the tradition of tapas in Spain.

We tend to spend time in Venice in the offseason, when the city is at its most quiet, mysterious, and beautiful. And also its most damp and dreary. It's easy to get lost in Venice, and few things in life are as comforting as finding a friendly spot in a narrow street where they serve you these delicious meatballs and a glass of simple wine.

NOTE

If the beef and potato mixture isn't holding its shape or seems too wet, add 2 more tablespoons breadcrumbs before shaping them into balls.

2 small russet potatoes, peeled

Fine sea salt and freshly ground black pepper

10 ounces / 300 g ground beef (80% lean)

1 ounce / 30 g mortadella, finely chopped

½ cup / 50 g grated Parmigiano Reggiano cheese

2 large eggs

2 sprigs of fresh parsley, finely chopped

1 garlic clove, minced

¼ teaspoon ground nutmeg

¾ cup / 75 g dried breadcrumbs

Vegetable oil, for frying

SERVES 4

1. Bring a medium pot of salted water to a boil over medium-high heat. Add the potatoes and cook until tender, 15 to 20 minutes. Drain, then return to the pot. Season with salt and pepper to taste and mash until smooth. Let cool for 10 minutes.

2. Once the potatoes have cooled, in a large bowl, combine the beef, mortadella, Parmigiano Reggiano, eggs, parsley, garlic, nutmeg, and mashed potatoes. Season with a teaspoon of salt and pepper. Shape into meatballs about 1½ inches / 4 cm in diameter.

3. Place the breadcrumbs in a shallow bowl and toss the meatballs in the breadcrumbs to coat.

4. Line a plate with paper towels. Pour 2 inches / 5 cm oil into a large, high-sided pan. Heat the oil to about 325°F / 160°C over medium-high heat. You can test whether the oil is hot enough by adding a pinch of breadcrumbs. If they brown within seconds, the oil is ready.

5. Working in batches, add the meatballs to the oil. Cook until golden on all sides, about 5 minutes. Place on the paper towel–lined plate to drain, then transfer to a serving plate and serve immediately.

One Page (or So) on Wine

by Oddur Thorisson

I love wine, but I rarely like to read about it. I'm not very much of a "look under the hood" type of guy. It's become very fashionable, or at least common, to educate yourself on wine. That's mostly positive. People—who twenty years ago would have asked the clerk at the wine store, "I need something that goes with steak," and would have been pointed toward something and been told, "Take that one, it's big. It's French," without a mention of the year, the region, or the maker—are now "experts" themselves. Some people refuse to drink anything but natural wine, yet they don't really know what it is. No one really does, not exactly. Others only want the "best." Whatever that is. Usually it means expensive. A famous label. Whether they'd recognize that wine in a lineup is another matter. Wine is wonderful and there are very few truths about it, but there are opinions. And those are personal, as they should be. The most important question to ask anyone tasting a wine is whether they like it. The second question could be why.

Mimi asked me to write about Italian wine for her last cookbook. I did, but it didn't end up in the book. If memory serves me, it was boring and judgmental, pompous even. Probably preachy. Thank god it didn't end up in the book. Mimi asked me again this time, and since it probably won't make the book, I'll keep it brief to save time, and if it does make the book, to save pages.

Italians have been creating wine forever. Most Italians drink wine with every dinner but often no more than a glass. Italians as a nation drink often but very little. Venetians and the winemakers themselves are the only general exceptions I know. Until recently, the wine culture in France was far more sophisticated than in Italy. Ordinary French people have been collecting wine for centuries, drinking from their grandparents' stock and filling it up for their children. A French high school teacher may not have a large salary, but he will somehow have a wine collection and be as familiar with the best years from certain regions as he is with the curriculum he's teaching.

Over here, wine was chiefly for the table. They talked about the food and washed it down with simple wine. Chianti was an unremarkable table wine. There were exceptions, the Brunellos of Tuscany, the Barolos of Piemonte, and the Amarones of Veneto, but the general public wasn't collecting them or probably even drinking them, at least not regularly. Such wines were for noble people to take out on special occasions, and even then, the year was an afterthought.

Wine wasn't a thing, but now it is.

Italians have long exported huge amounts of wine, but a lot of that has been of dubious quality, like mass-produced, cheap Prosecco, very simple whites, reds fit only for cooking, if that. In recent decades, the quality of Italian wines has been going rapidly upward. Regions that have always made good wine, like Piemonte, Tuscany, Veneto, and Sicily, have consistently upped their game. Other regions that weren't known for wine now are. Italy and its regions produce wine made from more indigenous varietals than any other country. Just pick any region and any village you want. Go to a good trattoria and ask for a great local bottle. They will have it, and while the name of the grape might be something you've never heard before, you will like it. Twenty years ago, they wouldn't even have had a wine list.

What is called natural wine has enjoyed singular success, not least in regions that weren't famous for wine (when you have nothing to lose, you can take more chances). The old guard is more resistant to change. Natural wine has to do with how the wine is made, mostly what is (or not) added. Organic is a different thing and has to do with the agriculture, whether pesticides were employed. A traditional wine can be organic but not natural. Most natural wine is also organic, which is logical. And calling classic wines traditional is misleading because the "natural" way is the original way, how wines were made before winemakers discovered certain, now controversial, techniques, like adding sulfites to stabilize the wine. My attitude to natural wine is that I like it if it's good. Not just because it's natural.

A type of Italian wine that's been on the rise is sparkling. Many people call all Italian sparkling wine Prosecco. But Prosecco is a particular type of bubbly that's produced only in the northeastern part of Italy, with specific grapes. The wines I'm talking about are called "Metodo Classico" (classic method) and are Champagne-style wines made in Italy, often using the same grapes as in France: Pinot Noir and Chardonnay, but also varieties specific to the region where they are made. The most famous of those wines are Franciacorta, which, like Champagne, is a place. Another well-known appellation is Alta Langa, here in Piemonte. They say that these wines are catching up and that some can now be compared in complexity to great Champagnes. It's almost true. Most important, the best ones are incredibly pleasant to drink and delicious.

It's dangerous to generalize too much about a subject like wine, but the rules of thumb, for me anyway, could be something like this. Good wines are now made everywhere in Italy. I would usually go for reds from the regions that have historically made good wines, like Piemonte and Tuscany. There are of course many exceptions nowadays (remember this is a rule of thumb, and we have only two of those). Nebbiolo (the grape used for Barolo) is my favorite of all. As for whites, I like Burgundies best. But they make great and diverse white wines everywhere in Italy, and for those, the rule of thumb is simply to try them all and drink what you like. And if you're in Italy, drink the wine that's most local. It's going to be good.

STRACCIATELLA ALLA ROMANA

Roman Egg Ribbon Soup

One of my favorite Italian soups and not to be confused with the chocolate-drizzled ice cream that it allegedly inspired or the creamy inside of a burrata cheese. In Italian the verb *stracciare* means "to shred" and here it refers to the eggs. I first had Stracciatella alla Romana, oddly enough, in New York, in a now-closed restaurant with wonderful zebra drawings on the walls and an old gentleman at the bar who was perfectly suited from the waist up but wearing tracksuit bottoms and sneakers. (He was drinking martinis, I remember, more than one.)

It's quite rare to find a stracciatella in restaurants, even in Rome, and if you ask for one, they inevitably think you are asking for the creamy shreds of Puglian cheese. We do, however, have it very frequently at home. It's equally appropriate as a light primi at a dinner party or when someone has a touch of a cold. You'll need good broth, which we usually have (on the stove or in the freezer), and the rest is so easy that the younger kids sometimes do it for themselves.

2 large carrots, sliced into 1½-inch / 4 cm pieces

1 celery rib, sliced into 1½-inch / 4 cm pieces

1 large white onion, quartered

1 teaspoon fine sea salt and 1 teaspoon freshly ground black pepper, plus more salt for seasoning

8 large eggs

6 tablespoons / 90 g grated Parmigiano Reggiano cheese

For serving

A few sprigs of fresh parsley, finely chopped

1 spring onion, finely chopped

Extra-virgin olive oil (optional)

SERVES 4 TO 6

1. In a large stockpot, combine the carrots, celery, and onion with 2 quarts / 2 liters water. Season generously with salt. Bring to a boil over high heat. Once boiling, reduce the heat to medium-low and simmer until the vegetables are tender, about 30 minutes.

2. Meanwhile, crack the eggs into a large bowl. Add the Parmigiano Reggiano and the salt and pepper. Beat the mixture until smooth and well combined.

3. Remove and discard the vegetables from the broth (a skimmer works well for this). Taste and season the broth with salt. Bring to a boil over high heat, then reduce the heat to low.

4. Slowly pour the beaten egg mixture into the boiling broth, whisking constantly, until ribbonlike strands form. The eggs will curl and streak, and you can break it up a bit with a wooden spoon. Remove the pot from the heat.

5. To serve, garnish with parsley, spring onion, and a drizzle of olive oil (if using).

RIBOLLITA TOSCANA

Tuscan Bread, Bean & Vegetable Soup

A soup so thick you can hardly call it that and the perfect foil for a cold winter's night. Wherever you are in the world, having this old peasant dish will transport you to a farmhouse in Tuscany where you can sit by the fire, enjoy a glass of local wine, and listen to the wind gently tickling the olive trees outside. This setting is vastly improved by the presence of a dog.

In Tuscany, they are known to use a lot of bread in their cooking. This has much to do with the fact that Tuscan bread is traditionally rather flavorless, unsalted (likely due to the taxation on salt in the olden days), and frankly not very exciting to eat on its own. One of the region's most famous dishes is pappa al pomodoro, a thick, tomato-based bread soup—the summer alternative to the ribollita of winter. Another bread-based dish is panzanella, a further example of using stale bread in a clever way and turning it into something tasty. The ribollita is really a meal on its own, but if you're planning to have a secondi, I suggest a small portion of this wonderful soup as it's very filling.

3 cups / 750 g canned cannellini beans (or 10 ounces / 300 g dried beans, soaked overnight), rinsed

1 sprig of fresh rosemary

5 tablespoons / 75 ml extra-virgin olive oil, plus more for garnish

1 medium red onion, chopped

2 carrots, diced

2 celery ribs, diced

2 medium potatoes, peeled and diced

2 teaspoons fresh thyme leaves

14 ounces / 400 g canned peeled tomatoes, chopped

7 ounces / 200 g Tuscan kale, chopped

7 ounces / 200 g Swiss chard, chopped

7 ounces / 200 g Savoy cabbage, chopped

7 cups / 1.6 liters vegetable stock, plus more as needed

4 slices stale rustic bread, crusts removed and cut into ½-inch / 1.25 cm pieces

Fine sea salt and freshly ground black pepper

Parmigiano Reggiano cheese, grated, for garnish

SERVES 6

1. If using dried beans, in a large pot, combine the beans and rosemary with 1 quart / liter water. Bring to a boil over medium-high heat, then reduce the heat to low and simmer gently until the beans are tender, 1 to 1½ hours. Remove half of the beans with a slotted spoon and add to a blender. Blend until you get a smooth and creamy paste. If using canned beans, add half of the beans to a blender until you get a smooth and creamy paste. Set aside.

2. In a large, heavy pot, heat the olive oil over medium heat. Add the onion, carrots, and celery and sauté, stirring frequently, until softened and slightly caramelized, about 5 minutes. Stir in the potatoes and thyme and cook until the potatoes are tender, 6 minutes more. Stir in the tomatoes and cook until they break down slightly, another 5 minutes.

3. Add the kale, Swiss chard, and cabbage and cook, stirring, until beginning to wilt, about 3 more minutes. Pour in enough vegetable stock (about 6 cups / 1.4 liters) to completely cover the vegetables and stir to combine.

recipe continues »

Ribollita Toscana CONTINUED

4. Bring the mixture to a boil over medium-high heat, then reduce the heat to low and simmer, stirring occasionally, for about 30 minutes, adding more stock as needed to keep the vegetables covered and to create the desired consistency. Stir in the pureed bean paste and cook until the soup is thickened, 25 more minutes.

5. Add the bread to the soup. Stir until the bread absorbs the liquid and starts dissolving, about 20 minutes more.

6. Stir in the whole beans and season with salt and pepper to taste, adding more stock if the soup seems too thick. Continue simmering until the soup has the desired thick consistency, about 10 minutes more.

7. Cover and leave to cool to room temperature. Refrigerate for at least 3 hours and up to overnight.

8. Reheat the soup gently before serving and adjust the seasoning if necessary.

9. Divide among serving bowls and top each serving with a drizzle of olive oil and grated Parmigiano Reggiano.

CRESPELLE AL FORNO

Baked Crepes

Before I moved to Italy, I wasn't really aware of the existence of Italian savory crepes, as I thought of them exclusively as part of the French cuisine. It turns out that Italians have their own pancake traditions, and many of the recipes bear a resemblance to cannelloni recipes. Some are stuffed with ricotta and spinach, while others like these—mostly in the North—are made with béchamel, butter, ham, and cheese (a French influence no doubt). After a full morning of skiing or a long walk in the hills, I can't think of anything more satisfying than to come back to the cabin for a lunch of these savory pancakes and a glass of good wine.

Crespelle

3 large eggs

1¾ cups / 210 g tipo "00" or all-purpose flour

Fine sea salt

2 cups / 500 ml whole milk

Unsalted butter, melted for greasing the pan

Filling

10 ounces / 300 g fresh mozzarella cheese

10 ounces / 300 g cooked ham

2 cups / 500 ml Béchamel (page 98)

Fine sea salt and freshly ground black pepper

½ cup / 50 g grated Parmigiano Reggiano cheese

SERVES 4

1. **Make the crespelle.** In a large bowl, beat the eggs until slightly frothy. Gradually sift the flour into the eggs, whisking continuously, until smooth. Add a pinch of salt. Slowly whisk in the milk until a smooth, lump-free batter forms.

2. Heat a medium crepe pan or nonstick skillet over medium heat. Brush the skillet with an even layer of butter.

3. Pour a ladleful of the batter into the center of the pan, then quickly tilt and rotate the pan to spread the batter into a thin, even layer.

4. Cook until the edges start to lift and the bottom is lightly golden, 1 to 2 minutes. Flip the crepe and cook 30 seconds to 1 minute more. Repeat with the remaining batter, brushing the pan with more butter as needed.

5. Preheat the oven to 400°F / 200°C.

6. **Make the filling.** In a medium bowl, fold the mozzarella and ham into 1 cup of the béchamel sauce. Season with salt and pepper.

7. Working one at a time, add a generous tablespoonful of the ham and cheese béchamel to the center of each crespelle. Roll or fold the crespelle over the sauce, then place, seam side down and tightly side by side, in a 9 × 13-inch / 23 × 33 cm baking dish. Pour the remaining 1 cup of béchamel over the crespelle and sprinkle with the Parmigiano Reggiano.

8. Bake until the sauce is bubbling and the crespelle are heated through, about 10 minutes. Turn the broiler on. Place the baking dish 4 to 6 inches / 10 to 15 cm under the broiler and broil until the top is golden and crisp, about 5 minutes (watch carefully). Remove the baking dish from the oven and let the crespelle cool for a few minutes before serving.

GNOCCHI ALLA ROMANA

Most people are familiar with potato gnocchi, which is served all over Italy, often with thick cheese sauces like Gorgonzola or Castelmagno, tomato sauces, or even ragù. Gnocchi alla Romana is a different type of dish, made without potatoes. They are prepared using semolina, milk, eggs, butter, and pecorino cheese, then baked until they have a golden, buttery crust. Some versions top the gnocchi with little meatballs, sausage bits, or ragù, but the most common, and perhaps the most authentic, version is without any of those. Gnocchi alla Romana are traditionally eaten as a first course (primi) in Rome, but I find they can also work very well as a side dish like polenta or as a part of a buffet meal.

1 quart / liter whole milk

2 teaspoons ground nutmeg

Fine sea salt and freshly ground black pepper

2 tablespoons / 30 g unsalted butter, cold

2 cups plus 1 tablespoon / 250 g semolina flour

2 large egg yolks

1 cup / 100 g grated Pecorino Romano cheese

3½ tablespoons / 50 g unsalted butter, melted

SERVES 4

1. Pour the milk into a large saucepan and season with the nutmeg, salt, and pepper. Add the 2 tablespoons / 30 g cold butter and bring to a simmer, stirring, over medium-low heat. Gradually add the semolina, stirring constantly, until fully incorporated. Remove from the heat and add the egg yolks and ¾ cup / 75 g of the cheese. Stir vigorously until well combined; it should have the consistency of cookie dough.

2. Cover a work surface with parchment paper. Transfer the dough to the parchment paper and divide in half. Roll each half into a tube (about 1½ inches / 4 cm thick) and wrap with the parchment paper. Let cool in the refrigerator to firm up for at least 40 minutes and up to 2 days.

3. Preheat the oven to 350°F / 180°C.

4. Slice the cooled rolls into ½-inch / 1 cm thick pieces using a smooth-blade knife.

5. Brush an 11-inch / 28 cm diameter (1¼-inch / 3 cm deep) round baking dish with half of the melted butter. Arrange the gnocchi in the dish, slightly overlapping. Brush the gnocchi with the remaining melted butter and sprinkle with the remaining 4 tablespoons / 25 g cheese.

6. Bake for about 15 minutes. Turn the broiler on. Broil 4 to 6 inches / 10 to 15 cm under the broiler until golden and bubbling, 2 to 3 minutes more.

SPAGHETTI ALL'ASSASSINA

This pasta has origins in Puglia, the heel of Italy, but the first time we had it was in a trattoria in Torino. We loved it—it's not unlike arrabbiata but with a different feel, more al dente and the sauce not quite like the spicy tomato sauces we are used to. We couldn't put our finger on it, but there had to be a secret technique. We asked the waiter and he unlocked the mystery. The pasta, he said, is cooked in the sauce, like a risotto, which explains the unfamiliar results.

It sounded simple enough to make, so we thought we'd try it at home. While we got there in the end, I must admit it took us a few attempts to get the assassina just right. I find this to be such an iconic dish. It brings to mind a stranger coming to a small town, sitting somewhere in a corner by himself, and asking only for a Spaghetti all'Assassina and a carafe of the house wine. When he is finished, he pays up, nods politely, and leaves, never to be seen again.

6 cups / 1.4 liters vegetable stock

6 tablespoons / 90 ml extra-virgin olive oil

3 garlic cloves, thinly sliced

1 pound / 500 g dried spaghettini

2 cups / 500 ml tomato passata

Fine sea salt

2 tablespoons crushed red pepper flakes

SERVES 4 TO 6

1. In a large saucepan, bring the stock to a simmer over medium-high heat. Reduce the heat to low to keep the stock at a simmer.

2. In a large, deep (preferably nonstick) sauté pan, heat the olive oil over medium heat. Once the oil is glistening, add the garlic and sauté until golden, about 2 minutes.

3. Add the spaghettini to the pan and spread it into an even layer. Pour the passata over the top, then immediately add enough warm stock to cover the spaghetti. Cook, gently stirring occasionally, until the pasta is softened and coated in sauce, about 6 minutes, adding more stock as needed to keep the spaghettini covered. Season with salt and the pepper flakes and continue cooking until al dente, about 6 more minutes. Serve immediately.

PASTA E FAGIOLI

This has to be one of the most heartwarming dishes in the book, because that's what it does: warms the heart and the soul on dark wintery nights. Various versions of this dish are cooked in many regions of Italy. The ingredients are easy to source and inexpensive, which makes this a very democratic recipe, affordable for everyone yet fit for a king. We have it often in Piemonte, but emotionally I connect pasta e fagioli with Naples. In local dialect, they call it "pasta e fasule," which turned into "pasta fazool" among Italian immigrants in America. "When the stars make you drool just like a pasta fazool, that's amore"—how can you not love that?

Pasta e fagioli is often served in a soup bowl, but different versions vary in both flavor and texture. I like mine a little on the soupier side, to be eaten with a spoon.

Pasta and beans is one of the most widespread dishes in the Italian tradition, belonging to the peasant cuisine found throughout the country, with many regional differences and variations.

10 ounces / 300 g dried borlotti beans, soaked overnight

2 bay leaves

2 tablespoons extra-virgin olive oil, plus more for garnish

1 medium onion, diced

1 celery rib, diced

1 carrot, diced

¼ cup / 60 ml tomato passata

Fine sea salt and freshly ground black pepper

5 ounces / 150 g dried ditalini or other small pasta

SERVES 4

1. Drain the beans and transfer to a large pot. Add the bay leaves and enough water to cover by 2 inches / 5 cm. Bring to a boil over high heat. Once boiling, reduce the heat to low and cover. Simmer until tender but not falling apart, about 1 hour. Reserving half of the bean water, drain the beans and discard the bay leaves.

2. In a large pot or Dutch oven, heat the olive oil over medium heat. Add the onion, celery, and carrot and sauté until softened and fragrant but not browned, 5 to 7 minutes. Reduce the heat to low. Stir in the tomato passata and cook until slightly reduced, about 5 more minutes.

3. Stir in the cooked beans and 2 cups / 500 ml of the reserved bean water. Season with salt and pepper to taste and cook until the flavors meld, about 15 minutes.

4. Remove half of the beans with a slotted spoon and add to a blender. Blend until you get a smooth and creamy paste. Use a spatula to scrape the puree back into the pot and add another 2 cups / 500 ml of the remaining reserved bean water. Increase the heat to medium, stir to combine, and bring to a boil.

5. Add the pasta and cook to al dente according to the package directions.

6. Serve with a drizzle of olive oil.

NEW YEAR'S EVE CAPELLINI *with* CAVIAR

When you choose recipes for a cookbook, you want to include what you love but also what you think will be most beneficial to your readers, the recipes they will fall in love with and may become staples in their homes. It's like when you are tidying up your closet, deciding what to keep and what to give away. Keeping the practical items is easy, but there will always be that dress or suit that you haven't worn for a long time and are not sure you ever will. You choose to keep it anyway because it would be too sad if you one day decided to wear it and the dress was no longer there.

This dish is like that. My husband kept talking about this Italian cookbook he had in his early twenties but no longer owns. Apparently it was some sort of bible that can't be found anywhere except in the halls of his memory. In it was a recipe that he never got around to making, which he always regretted, a New Year's Eve angel hair pasta with caviar. So I did some research and some tests and came up with this one. We've had it a few times and it's really good, but it's hardly become an everyday staple. I'm not throwing it out, though. One day when all the kids are gone, it will be just me and him, black tie and long dress, sitting in the kitchen on New Year's Eve, drinking Champagne, and having this pasta.

1 pound / 500 g dried capellini

2 tablespoons / 30 g unsalted butter

1 tablespoon lemon juice

½ cup / 120 ml dry white wine

¾ cup / 180 ml heavy cream

Fine sea salt and freshly ground black pepper

2 ounces / 60 g caviar

SERVES 4

1. Bring a large pot of salted water to a boil over high heat. Add the pasta and cook to al dente according to the package directions. Reserving 1 cup / 250 ml of the pasta water, drain the pasta.

2. Meanwhile, in a large skillet, melt the butter over medium heat. Add the lemon juice and wine and cook, stirring, until evaporated, about 1 minute. Stir in the cream and bring to a simmer until slightly thickened, about 5 minutes.

3. Add the pasta and toss until well coated, adding pasta water to loosen the sauce if needed. Season with salt and pepper. Divide among serving plates, top each with a spoonful of caviar, and serve immediately.

PENNE ALLA VODKA

Easily the most '80s dish in the book and also one of my favorites. I was a teenager in the '80s, and I still love the music, the movies, the fashion, the big hair, and all the bling. The origins of this pasta are wildly disputed, but it was a top seller both in the United States and Italy at the same time. While this disco pasta faded into obscurity in the decades that followed, it's been having a resurgence lately, maybe thanks to social media.

One year, we had a holiday in Filicudi just as Italy had begun to open up carefully at the tail end of the pandemic lockdown. We were practically the only people around as we found our way south, through Florence and empty Rome until we arrived in Sicily. From there, we took a boat, driven by the owner of the house we were renting. He promised us dolphins, swimming, and fishing on the way. Instead, we hit a bad storm and arrived soaked and shaken at the harbor of the island. Carlo, the owner, was very sorry and wanted to get us anything we needed to forget about the traumatic passage. I asked for a bottle of vodka. He understood perfectly. When he brought it to the house and I started cooking with the vodka instead of drinking it, his jaw dropped. A playboy in the '80s, he hadn't thought of penne alla vodka for decades. After that, he saw us in a different light, blasts from the past.

5½ tablespoons / 80 g unsalted butter

1 small onion, finely chopped

Pinch of crushed red pepper flakes

1 cup / 230 g tomato puree

½ cup / 120 ml vodka

½ cup / 120 ml heavy cream

Fine sea salt

1 pound / 500 g dried penne pasta

1 ounce / 30 g Parmigiano Reggiano cheese, grated

SERVES 4 TO 6

1. In a large saucepan, melt the butter over medium heat. Add the onion and pepper flakes and sauté until golden, about 4 minutes.

2. Reduce the heat to low. Add the tomato puree and cook until simmering, about 3 minutes. Stir in the vodka and cook until evaporated and reduced, about 15 minutes. Add the cream and stir gently. Season with salt.

3. Meanwhile, bring a large pot of salted water to a boil over high heat. Add the pasta and cook to al dente according to the package directions. Drain the pasta.

4. Add the pasta to the sauce. Increase the heat to high and cook, tossing until thoroughly coated, about 1 minute. Serve immediately, sprinkled with the cheese.

TAGLIOLINI *alla* GRANSEOLA

Tagliolini with Spider Crab

I've always loved seafood platters, and over the years, I've become something of an expert in removing the flesh of various crustaceans from their shells. It's messy but delicious. We had an abundance of seafood in Hong Kong, where I grew up, and on trips to my mother's native France, our first stop was always La Coupole, the legendary brasserie in Montparnasse. My father loved to order the "royal seafood platter" even if he didn't actually plan to eat much of it himself—I guess he just liked the visual. So I sat there, a little girl breaking claws, peeling shrimp for my mother, while my parents ate their sole meunière.

Nowadays, this particular skill means that every time we order seafood, the kids just gently pass their plates to me and let me do the work. I'm particularly fond of spider crab, and while the slightly tender meat needs no more than a squeeze of lemon to be thoroughly enjoyed, I find it works incredibly well with delicate pasta recipes, especially with fresh pasta like tagliolini. Female spider crabs are celebrated in the culinary world for their rich and robust flavor, enhancing dishes like pasta with remarkable depth. Their roe, or coral, brings a luxurious, creamy texture and a unique taste to sauces, transforming the dish into an extraordinary experience.

¼ cup / 60 ml extra-virgin olive oil

3 garlic cloves, minced

12 ounces / 350 g spider crabmeat and the additional coral

Fine sea salt and freshly ground black pepper

¼ cup / 60 ml brandy

½ cup / 120 ml fish stock

½ cup / 75 g cherry tomatoes, halved

¼ cup / 60 ml heavy cream

1 pound / 500 g fresh tagliolini pasta

¼ cup / 15 g chopped fresh parsley

SERVES 4

1. In a large skillet, heat the olive oil over medium heat. Add the garlic and sauté until fragrant and golden, about 2 minutes. Add the crabmeat and coral and cook until heated through and slightly golden, about 3 minutes. Season with salt and pepper.

2. Pour in the brandy, then tilt the pan away from you and carefully ignite the alcohol to flambé. Once the flames subside, add the stock and cherry tomatoes and cook, stirring gently, until simmering, about 5 minutes. Stir in the cream and cook until slightly thickened, 2 to 3 minutes.

3. Meanwhile, bring a large pot of salted water to a boil over high heat. Add the pasta and cook to al dente according to the package directions. Reserving 1 cup / 250 ml of the pasta water, drain the pasta.

4. Add the pasta and toss until well combined, adding pasta water to loosen the sauce if needed. Taste and season with more salt and pepper if needed. Serve immediately, garnished with the parsley.

TREVISO & TALEGGIO LASAGNA

Veneto, the region of Venice, is all about seafood—the Veneto coastline stretches over 93 miles (150 km) along the Adriatic Sea—but they have a few other signature dishes and ingredients that are equally emblematic of the region. To me, Veneto will always be synonymous with the radicchio Tardivo di Treviso, considered the king of all radicchio in Italy and the product of meticulous and very specific, traditional growing methods. The Treviso Tardivo is one of the most beautiful vegetables I know, rivaling even zucchini flowers in terms of sheer beauty. This is a great alternative to other more meat-heavy lasagnas when you're in the mood for something hearty and comforting but would like to take a break from meat or fish. Taleggio is a cheese made all over northeastern Italy, originating near Bergamo in Lombardia, but also made in Treviso, where the radicchio comes from, so it made sense to use them together

3 tablespoons extra-virgin olive oil, plus more for greasing the pan

2 shallots, finely chopped

1½ pounds / 700 g Treviso radicchio, thinly sliced

Fine sea salt and freshly ground black pepper

3 ounces / 90 g Parmigiano Reggiano cheese, grated

2 cups / 500 ml Béchamel (page 98)

8 ounces / 250 g fresh lasagna sheets

7 ounces / 200 g Taleggio cheese, sliced

SERVES 4

1. Preheat the oven to 350°F / 180°C. Grease a 9 × 13-inch / 23 × 33 cm baking dish with olive oil.

2. In a large skillet, heat the olive oil over medium heat. Add the shallots and sauté until softened, 3 minutes.

3. Add the radicchio and cook until golden, 10 minutes. Season with salt and pepper. Remove from the heat and let cool for 5 minutes.

4. In a large bowl, combine the radicchio, half the Parmigiano Reggiano, and the béchamel.

5. Add a single layer of lasagna sheets on the bottom of the prepared dish. Top with a third each of the béchamel mixture and Taleggio, then sprinkle with some of the remaining Parmigiano Reggiano. Repeat the process twice. Bake until bubbly and golden, about 25 minutes. Let cool for 10 minutes before serving.

L'Etal du Boucher

LASAGNA BOLOGNESE

Everyone I know loves lasagna. Even a mediocre one is still pretty good; there's just something about lasagna that makes it tasty and satisfying (almost) every time. Call it the baked-in-the-oven effect. A Bolognese ragù has little to no tomato, and neither does a real Lasagna Bolognese. The universal rendition, the one you get in Italian restaurants around the world, is almost a hybrid. It's tomatoey, the pasta sheets tend to be on the thicker side, and so on. It's good, but it's, shall we say, international. Because lasagna is everywhere, I think people sometimes take it for granted. You're always up for a lasagna, but it's not necessarily what you'd plan for Christmas.

One reason may be that people in general simply haven't had a real Lasagna Bolognese the way it should be made, and is made in Bologna every day. There is a scene in my favorite food movie, *Big Night*, where the brother who's the chef, Primo, talks about Lasagna Bolognese: "It's so good that after you have it you have to kill yourself." I don't quite relate, but I get what he means. A well-made Lasagna Bolognese (and I hope this recipe does the dish justice) is a true contender for the best food in the world.

6 tablespoons / 90 ml extra-virgin olive oil, plus more for greasing

1 large onion, finely chopped

1 carrot, finely chopped

1 celery rib, finely chopped

3½ ounces/ 100 g pancetta, finely chopped

8 ounces / 250 g ground veal

8 ounces / 250 g ground pork

⅔ cup / 150 ml red wine

1½ cups / 350 ml tomato passata

1 cup / 250 ml beef stock

Fine sea salt and freshly ground black pepper

3½ tablespoons / 50 g unsalted butter

½ cup / 120 ml whole milk

12 to 15 Spinach Lasagna Sheets (recipe follows)

2 cups / 500 ml Béchamel (page 98)

1 cup / 100 g grated Parmigiano Reggiano cheese

SERVES 4

1. In a large, heavy pot, heat 2 tablespoons of the olive oil over medium heat. Add the onion, carrot, and celery and sauté until the vegetables are softened and the onion is translucent, 5 to 7 minutes. Add the pancetta and cook, stirring occasionally, until lightly browned and crispy, about 5 more minutes.

2. Increase the heat to medium-high and add the remaining olive oil. Add the veal and pork and cook, breaking up the meat with a wooden spoon, until browned, about 8 minutes. Add the wine and cook until mostly evaporated, 3 to 5 minutes. Stir in the passata and stock. Season with salt and pepper. Add the butter and milk and reduce the heat to low. Cover and cook, stirring occasionally and adding a splash of water if needed, until you get a smooth and rich sauce, about 2 hours. Adjust the seasoning.

3. Preheat the oven to 350°F / 180°C. Lightly grease a 9 × 13-inch / 23 × 33 cm baking dish with olive oil.

4. Bring a large pot of salted water to a boil over high heat. Add the lasagna and stir the sheets gently to prevent them from sticking together and cook to al dente, about 1 minute. Drain the pasta and rinse under cold water. Lay out flat on a baking sheet or parchment paper.

5. Spread a thin layer of sauce on the bottom of the prepared baking dish. Add a single layer of the lasagna sheets over top. Spread with a thin layer of béchamel, then spoon a generous amount of sauce over top and sprinkle with Parmigiano Reggiano. Repeat the process three times, until the dish is nearly full. Bake until bubbly, golden, and crispy around the edges, 25 to 30 minutes. Let cool for about 10 minutes before serving.

Spinach Lasagna Sheets

Makes 12 to 15 sheets

5 ounces / 150 g fresh spinach (or use frozen spinach, thawed and well drained)

1½ cups / 180 g all-purpose flour, plus more for dusting

2 large eggs

Pinch of fine sea salt

1. If using fresh spinach, bring a large pot of salted water to a boil over high heat. Add the spinach and cook until wilted and tender, 2 to 3 minutes. Using a slotted spoon, transfer the spinach to a fine-mesh sieve. Press out as much moisture as possible. Spread the spinach out on a plate and let cool completely.

2. Transfer the cooled spinach (or well-drained thawed spinach) to a food processor and pulse until very finely chopped but not quite smooth.

3. Mound the flour on a work surface. Make a well in the center of the flour and add the eggs, chopped spinach, and salt. Using a fork, beat the eggs gently with the spinach. Slowly incorporate the flour, starting with the inner sides of the well.

4. When the dough begins to come together, start kneading using just your palms with a back-and-forth motion (the joke is that you should always be able to answer the phone while making pasta!), 8 to 10 minutes. Use a dough scraper to scrape away any stray bits around the pasta dough, as dried-out dough will interfere with your pasta and make it lumpy. The dough is ready when it is elastic and the surface gently "comes back to you" when pressed. If the dough gets too sticky, sprinkle with flour as you knead.

5. Form the dough into a ball and wrap it tightly in plastic wrap. Let the dough rest at room temperature for about 1 hour. This will allow the dough to relax and make the dough more elastic and easier to work with.

6. When ready to roll out the dough, dust a work surface and rolling pin lightly with flour. Cut off a piece of dough (the equivalent of a handful), press with your palm onto the work surface, and roll out with the rolling pin to about ½ inch / 1 cm thick. Set a pasta machine to its thickest setting and roll the pasta dough through it.

7. Switch the pasta machine to the next thinnest setting and roll the pasta dough through again. Continue switching the settings lower and lower until you get a thin and perfectly smooth sheet of pasta, about dial 7. Repeat with the remaining dough.

8. Place one of the pasta sheets on the work surface. Cut into 4 × 8-inch / 10 × 20 cm lasagna sheets and repeat with the remaining pasta.

BROILED SCALLOPS *with* RADICCHIO, BÉCHAMEL & TALEGGIO

Earlier I called the radicchio Tardivo di Treviso one of the most beautiful vegetables in the world. Likewise, scallops are one of the most beautiful things to come out of the sea. Combining them in one recipe is truly a tale of two beauties. The result: the most decadent, heavenly scallops bubbling with the rich combination of Taleggio and béchamel sauce.

This is one of my go-to dishes when I'm hosting a dinner party and I want the menu to be a little fancy. I like to lay the scallops in their shells on a tray next to an abundance of the Treviso (I can never resist buying too much), and together they illuminate the kitchen like a painting. I alternate between serving these scallops as a small starter (one per person) or as a main after a good primi (three to five for each guest).

2 tablespoons extra-virgin olive oil

12 ounces / 340 g Treviso radicchio, finely chopped

¾ cup / 180 ml Béchamel (page 98)

8 raw sea scallops on the half shell

Fine sea salt and freshly ground black pepper

3 tablespoons dry white wine

8 slices Taleggio cheese

SERVES 2

1. In a large sauté pan, heat the olive oil over medium heat. Add the radicchio and sauté until golden, 4 to 5 minutes.

2. In a medium bowl, combine the radicchio with the béchamel.

3. Season the scallops (in their shells) lightly with salt and pepper and sprinkle with the wine. Top each scallop with about 1½ tablespoons of the béchamel mixture and a slice of Taleggio. Season with salt and pepper.

4. Preheat the broiler. Place the scallops on a baking tray 4 to 6 inches / 10 to 15 cm under the broiler and broil until the cheesy sauce is golden and bubbling, 8 to 10 minutes (watch carefully). Serve immediately.

PORK SAUSAGE *with* BROCCOLI RABE

If you spend time in Naples, you will no doubt have a pizza. It is undeniable that the most popular version remains the Margherita and her spinoffs—with cherry tomatoes, bufala mozzarella, and so forth—but you will soon notice that most pizzerias also offer the combination of sausage and friarielli, what we call broccoli rabe in English or cime di rapa in northern Italy. This bitter, green, cruciferous vegetable is widely used in Italian cooking, and in Campania, they love to pair it with pork. This combination is everywhere, particularly when it comes to casual or street food; various sandwiches with pork and friarielli are a staple of the local cuisine.

I tend to cook this recipe most in winter, typically on a weeknight when something hearty, healthy, and filling is needed.

3.3 pounds / 1.5 kg broccoli rabe, tough stems removed

6 tablespoons / 90 ml extra-virgin olive oil

2 garlic cloves, crushed

2 dried red chile peppers, crushed

1¾ pounds / 800 g pork sausage

½ cup / 120 ml dry white wine

Fine sea salt and freshly ground black pepper

SERVES 4

1. Set up a bowl of ice water. Bring a large pot of lightly salted water to a boil over high heat. Add the broccoli rabe and cook until tender, 3 minutes. Transfer to the ice water bath to stop the cooking. Drain well.

2. In a large sauté pan, heat 4 tablespoons / 60 ml of the olive oil over medium heat. Add 1 garlic clove and the chiles and sauté until the oil is infused, about 3 minutes. Add the blanched broccoli rabe and sauté until fragrant, about 10 more minutes.

3. In a separate large sauté pan, heat the remaining 2 tablespoons olive oil over medium heat. Add the sausages and remaining garlic clove and cook, turning regularly, until the sausage is browned on all sides, about 5 minutes. Add the wine and let it evaporate. Reduce the heat to low, cover, and cook until cooked through, about 10 minutes.

4. Transfer the cooked sausages to the pan with the broccoli rabe and toss everything together to combine the flavors. Season with a little salt and pepper. Serve immediately.

NORTHERN ITALIAN GOULASH *with* POLENTA

I keep returning to the subject of the incredible diversity of Italian cooking. Dishes they've never even heard of in the North are everywhere in the South. The regionality is particularly noticeable in border areas such as the northeastern region of Italy, Friuli-Venezia Giulia, which shares borders with Austria and Slovenia. It seems the locals prefer to speak German or Slovenian over Italian, or at least are fine with either. The houses look right out of Hansel and Gretel, as do many of the outfits. Let's just say this is not the Italy of Vespas, gelato, and dark-haired men with slicked-back hair in shiny suits drinking Americanos. This is polenta and grappa country, with a healthy dose of goulash. We once stayed in a hotel near both the Slovenian and Austrian borders. They served us a risotto with radicchio and then a delicious goulash to follow, which I always remembered and have made variations of at home since then.

Italian versions usually have a hint of tomato, like we do here, but often do not include any carrots or celery. But I think a goulash needs carrots, so I added a couple. Serving this dish with a polenta makes it feel distinctively Alpine Italian.

3½ tablespoons / 50 g unsalted butter

4½ tablespoons / 60 ml extra-virgin olive oil

2 pounds / 1 kg white onions, thinly sliced

2 carrots, sliced into ½-inch / 1.25 cm thick rounds

2 pounds / 1 kg beef shoulder, cut into 1½-inch / 3 cm chunks

4 juniper berries

2½ tablespoons all-purpose flour

¼ cup / 50 ml red wine

1¼ cups / 300 ml beef stock

2 tablespoons tomato paste

2 teaspoons sweet paprika

1 teaspoon hot paprika

Polenta

4 cups / 950 ml water or stock (vegetable or chicken stock for extra flavor)

Fine sea salt and freshly ground black pepper

1 cup / 150 g instant polenta

2 tablespoons / 30 g unsalted butter

½ cup / 50 g grated Parmigiano Reggiano cheese (optional but recommended)

SERVES 4 TO 6

1. In a large Dutch oven, heat the butter and olive oil over medium heat until the butter has melted. Add the onions and cook until softened and translucent, 8 minutes. Add the carrots and sauté until golden, 3 more minutes. Add the beef and cook, stirring, until browned on all sides, about 6 minutes. Add the juniper berries and sprinkle the beef with the flour; stir well to coat.

2. Add the wine and deglaze the pan, stirring constantly and scraping up all of the browned bits. Stir in the stock, tomato paste, sweet paprika, and hot paprika. Bring to a boil, then reduce the heat to low, cover, and simmer, stirring occasionally, until the beef is tender and the flavors have melded, 1½ to 2 hours.

3. **Make the polenta.** In a medium saucepan, bring the water or stock to a boil over medium-high heat. Add a pinch of salt for seasoning. Once the liquid is boiling, slowly pour in the polenta, whisking continuously to avoid lumps. It should begin to thicken quickly. Reduce the heat to low and continue stirring until the polenta has thickened to your desired consistency, 2 to 3 minutes. Stir in the butter and Parmigiano Reggiano (if using). This will add creaminess and flavor to the polenta. Taste and adjust the seasoning with more salt and pepper as needed.

4. Spoon the polenta into bowls or onto plates. Serve immediately with the goulash.

BUGIE DI CARNEVALE

Carnival Fritters

Italians have a range of dishes for each of their numerous holidays, not least in the sweets department. Many pastries and cakes are dedicated to Easter and Christmas, but around Carnival, every pastry shop is filled with these delicious fried and crumbly delights, sprinkled in abundance with powdered sugar. In Piemonte, they are called bugie, which translates into "lies," or rather "sweet little lies," but in other regions they have various other names and versions. Good-quality bugie is easy to find in February, so I don't really have to make them myself, but in a similar way as with madeleines, nothing beats the feeling of a homemade bugie, still warm from frying and dusted with powdered sugar.

1. In a large bowl, combine the flour, butter, granulated sugar, eggs, lemon zest, and wine until a smooth dough forms. Knead the dough until homogeneous. Wrap the dough in plastic wrap and chill in the refrigerator for 30 minutes to rest.

2. Sprinkle a little flour on a clean work surface and roll out the dough with a rolling pin to about ¹⁄₁₆ inch / 2 mm thick. Cut the dough into rectangles about 4 inches / 10 cm long and 2 inches / 5 cm wide.

3. Line a baking sheet with paper towels. Pour 2 inches / 5 cm oil into a large, high-sided pan. Heat the oil to about 350°F / 180°C over medium heat. You can test whether the oil is hot enough by adding in a small drop of batter. If it sizzles and turns golden and crisp, the oil is ready. Working in batches, deep-fry the rectangles, flipping occasionally, until golden and crisp, 1 to 2 minutes. Transfer to the paper towel–lined baking sheet to drain, then dust generously with powdered sugar. Serve warm.

2½ cups / 300 g all-purpose flour, plus more for dusting

3½ tablespoons / 50 g unsalted butter, softened at room temperature

¼ cup / 50 g granulated sugar

2 large eggs

Grated zest of 1 lemon

2 tablespoons dry white wine or Marsala wine

Vegetable oil, for frying

Powdered sugar, for dusting

MAKES ABOUT 22 FRITTERS

STRUFFOLI

Neapolitan Honey Balls

The very first time I visited Naples was in early December many years ago. After I had satisfied my cravings for fried pizza and sfogliatelle, I started paying attention to these marvelous, marble-size honey balls that I would see on the counter of every pastry store. The name was so enticing, the pastries so glistening and old-fashioned. We bought a few, and while they were very good, I found them somewhat underwhelming. Since then, they've grown on me, and I have found that the real magic lies in making them at home and arranging them into a beautiful pyramid or a doughnut, almost like making a gingerbread house, but more original and attractive. Having a shapely struffoli arrangement in our kitchen has become an important part of our holiday preparations, and I no longer find them underwhelming at all. They are always on the menu—we snack on them when we want, and they go well with anything from the morning coffee to Champagne in the early evenings.

Dough

2 cups / 240 g all-purpose flour, plus more for dusting

3 large eggs

Pinch of fine sea salt

8 tablespoons / 110 grams unsalted butter, softened

2 tablespoons / 30 ml dark rum

Grated zest of ½ lemon

Grated zest of ½ orange

Vegetable oil, for frying

Honey Syrup

⅔ cup / 160 ml honey

1 tablespoon lemon juice

½ cup / 100 g granulated sugar

¾ cup / 60 g diced candied orange peel

¾ cup / 60 g diced candied lemon peel

A few tablespoons of multicolored sprinkles

SERVES 6

1. **Make the dough.** Sift the flour into a large bowl. Make a well in the center and add the eggs, salt, butter, rum, and zests. Mix to form a smooth dough, kneading thoroughly. Wrap the dough in plastic wrap and let it rest in the refrigerator for at least 1 hour or up to overnight to firm up.

2. Sprinkle a little flour on a clean work surface and roll out the dough into thick ropes, about ¼ inch / 6 mm thick. Cut into ¼-inch / 6 mm portions and roll each into a ball. Transfer to a baking sheet and lightly dust the dough balls with flour.

3. Line a baking sheet with paper towels. Pour 2 inches / 5 cm vegetable oil into a large, high-sided pan. Heat the oil to about 325°F / 160°C over medium heat. You can test whether the oil is hot enough by dropping a pinch of dough into the oil. If the dough turns golden within seconds, the oil is ready. Working in batches, deep-fry the balls until golden and puffy, 1 to 2 minutes. Transfer to the paper towel–lined baking sheet to drain.

4. **Make the honey syrup.** In a large saucepan, combine the honey, lemon juice, and sugar. Cook over medium heat, stirring, until combined and bubbling, about 5 minutes. Remove from the heat. Add the struffoli and half the candied peels and toss until evenly coated with the glaze. Transfer to a serving plate and pile the balls high.

5. Before serving, scatter the sprinkles and remaining candied peels over top.

ALMOND & ORANGE GELATO

I'm more of a gelato girl than I like to admit. Once in a while in Torino I will take the kids across our piazza, ostensibly because they want ice cream, when the real reason is that Mamma wants one for herself. This is a manageable craving that strikes only so often, just one of those things that brighten up a dull day. It gets more complicated when I'm in Naples or in Procida, where we spend our summer holidays. My absolute favorite ice cream in the world is the almond and orange gelato they sell at Mennella in Naples.

One day last summer during our vacation in Procida, with scorching temperatures and high humidity, so hot that the kids were not sure they could brave the short trek to the beach, I decided to go to Naples for the day simply because I couldn't stop thinking about my Mennella gelato. After a bus, boat, and taxi I stood there, satisfied for a few minutes, the happiest girl in Naples. Then another taxi, boat, and bus, and I arrived drenched at our doorstep, about five hours after I left. "Enough is enough," I thought to myself. That was the week I started making a version of my beloved gelato at home.

Almonds

⅔ cup / 100 g unsalted almonds, chopped

2 tablespoons / 30 g unsalted butter, melted

Gelato

2 cups / 500 ml heavy whipping cream

¼ cup / 60 ml honey

One 14-ounce / 400 g can sweetened condensed milk

1 teaspoon vanilla bean paste

Grated zest of 1 large orange

¾ cup / 60 g diced candied orange peel

SERVES 4 TO 6

1. Preheat the oven to 350°F / 180°C.

2. **Make the almonds.** In a small bowl, combine the almonds and melted butter until evenly coated. Spread on a small baking sheet in an even layer and bake for about 10 minutes, stirring twice, until golden and fragrant. Remove from the oven and let cool to room temperature.

3. **Make the gelato.** In the bowl of a stand mixer fitted with the whisk attachment, combine the cream, honey, sweetened condensed milk, vanilla bean paste, and orange zest. Whip until stiff peaks form. Gently fold in the cooled almonds and candied orange.

4. Transfer the mixture to a loaf pan or another freezer-safe container and smooth into an even layer. Cover with plastic wrap or a lid. Freeze until the mixture is firm, at least 6 hours, then serve.

WHITE CHOCOLATE PISTACHIO COOKIES

December is the month of baking on the weekends, and for the last few years, these absolutely terrific white chocolate pistachio cookies have been the bestseller in our house—everyone loves them. I try to make a batch that will tide us over until the next weekend's baking session, but we rarely get past Tuesday. These cookies are of Sicilian origin, and I do my best to use only the very best pistachios, straight from Sicily, as it makes all the difference. Another famous Sicilian export, mandarins and clementines, are at their peak around Christmas, so an afternoon snack of pairing the cookies and the citrus is as lovely as it gets.

1⅓ cups / 190 g shelled, unsalted pistachios

½ cup / 100 g granulated sugar

⅔ cup / 70 g almond flour

1½ teaspoons honey

½ teaspoon vanilla extract

1 tablespoon grated lemon zest

1 large egg white

1 cup / 170 g white chocolate chips

⅓ cup / 40 g powdered sugar, sifted

MAKES 24 COOKIES

1. Preheat the oven to 350°F / 175°C. Line a large baking sheet with parchment paper.

2. In a food processor, pulse the pistachios with ¼ cup / 50 g of the granulated sugar until coarsely ground. Be careful not to grind them too fine.

3. Transfer the pistachio mixture to a large bowl. Add the remaining ¼ cup / 50 g granulated sugar, the almond flour, honey, vanilla, and lemon zest and whisk to combine. Add the egg white and mix until the dough holds its shape when pressed together. Gently fold in the chocolate chips.

4. Place the powdered sugar in a small bowl. Form the dough into 1¼-inch / 3 cm balls in your palm, then roll in the powdered sugar. Place the dough balls about 2 inches / 5 cm apart on the prepared baking sheet. Dip the bottom of a cup in the powdered sugar (to help prevent sticking), then use it to press down the ball until it's about 2 inches / 5 cm wide.

5. Bake for 7 to 10 minutes. You want the cookie to retain its green color and not toast the pistachios too much. You will get a lovely chewy cookie. Remove from the oven and let cool before serving.

CHRISTMAS EVE *with the* THORISSONS

THE CHRISTMAS HOLIDAY PERIOD and all the feasts that go with it stretch out over several days in our house, as I'm sure they do in many other households. We are a multicultural family: I grew up in Hong Kong, which in those days followed British Christmas traditions, but my mother is French, so we always maintained a strong bond with the French ways of doing things as well. My husband is Icelandic and celebrates a bit differently, being Lutheran. And finally, we live in Italy, where they have their own way of celebrating.

In Iceland, Christmas Eve is the night of the biggest celebrations. That's when they open all the presents and have the most important meal of the holidays, while the twenty-fifth is a day for meeting the extended family—still very festive but not the main event. In our family, we stick to this preference for the twenty-fourth. That's when we open presents and put our very finest foot forward. Italian tradition dictates that there should be no meat on the twenty-fourth, which comes from the Roman Catholic tradition; since meat will be had in abundance on the twenty-fifth, you should abstain from it the night before. We try to stick to that rule because we like to adapt to local traditions and we love seafood. Then we have a lineup of menus that will follow in the days to come. On Christmas Day, we might stick to northern Italian traditions and have tortellini in broth or agnolotti, then a stuffed capon. Or we might go a little British, and I'll make a beef Wellington. With all the mishmash, maybe a shrimp cocktail to start. (One of the days, usually the twenty-sixth, we will do a Russian menu, borscht and beef stroganoff, but that's another story.)

Here is our Christmas Eve menu. I've tweaked it over the years, and I think now it's perfect, for us at least. I wouldn't be surprised if we never change it again.

FRIED SPAGHETTI-WRAPPED SHRIMP

I discovered these very fun and festive sticks in Naples, and I've been making them ever since. We used to start our Christmas meals with a classic shrimp cocktail, but these are so crunchy and good, and the kids find them exhilarating.

8 ounces / 225 g dried spaghetti

12 large shrimp, peeled, deveined, and butterflied

Wooden skewer sticks, about 10 inches / 25 cm long

¾ cup / 100 g all-purpose flour

1 teaspoon baking powder

½ teaspoon fine sea salt

¼ cup / 50 ml ice-cold water

Vegetable oil, for frying

Fine sea salt and freshly ground black pepper

½ cup / 100 ml mayonnaise

Juice of ½ lemon

Lemon wedges, for serving

SERVES 6

1. Bring a large pot of salted water to a boil over high heat. Add the pasta and cook to al dente according to the package directions. Drain the pasta and divide it into 12 even portions.

2. Wrap each portion of spaghetti around 1 shrimp and press firmly so it all sticks together. Ensure the shrimp are securely wrapped and place a stick in the center of the shrimp and pasta, making sure to secure everything together to prevent unraveling during frying.

3. In a medium bowl, whisk together the flour, baking powder, salt, and ice-cold water until smooth and thick enough to coat the back of a spoon.

4. Line a large plate with paper towels. Pour 2 inches / 5 cm oil into a large, high-sided pan. Heat the oil to about 350°F / 180°C over medium-high heat. You can test whether the oil is hot enough by adding in a small piece of bread. If it sizzles and turns golden and crisp, the oil is ready. Working in batches, and adding one at a time, dip the wrapped shrimp into the batter, then immediately transfer it to the oil to fry until golden brown and crispy, 3 to 4 minutes. Transfer to the paper towel–lined plate to drain. Season with salt and pepper.

5. In a small bowl, combine the mayonnaise and lemon juice.

6. Serve the fried shrimp on sticks with the sauce on the side for dipping along with the lemon wedges.

LOBSTER & PASTA SOUP

While on holiday in Marsala, Sicily, we had lunch at a highly rated but simple trattoria called Da Pino. I wasn't expecting anything out of the ordinary, but when I noticed a lobster soup with pasta (short capellini or short spaghettini) on the menu, my anticipation increased rapidly. After the first few spoons, I announced it to be "the best thing I've ever had." Admittedly I've said that a few times before and after, but it comes from the heart, and I mean it every time. This is a contender for the last meal I'll ever have, the kind of food I dream of. This is the most important part of our Christmas dinner. The flavor of the broth is extraordinary; the lobster pieces are irresistible. The fine little pasta floating around appeals to the child in all of us and brings back memories of various soups with noodles or pasta, which is perfect on Christmas Eve.

4 tablespoons / 60 ml extra-virgin olive oil, plus more for garnish

1 white onion, finely chopped

2 tablespoons tomato paste

6 cups / 1.5 liters hot water

40 basil leaves, plus a little extra for garnish

2 garlic cloves, peeled

2 lobsters, cut into pieces (claws, tail, and body)

1 cup / 250 ml dry white wine

Fine sea salt and freshly ground black pepper

6 ounces/ 170 g short angel hair pasta or vermicelli, broken into 1-inch / 2.5 cm lengths

1 teaspoon crushed red pepper flakes

SERVES 4

1. In a large saucepan, heat 2 tablespoons of the olive oil over medium heat. Add the onion and sauté until golden brown, about 4 minutes. Stir in the tomato paste and cook for about 2 minutes. Gradually add 3 cups / 750 ml of the hot water, stirring continuously, until combined. Reduce the heat to low and simmer until the sauce has thickened and is bubbly, about 10 minutes.

2. Meanwhile, in a food processor, combine the basil and garlic and pulse until finely chopped. Add the remaining 2 tablespoons olive oil and pulse a few more times to combine.

3. Stir the basil-garlic mixture into the tomato mixture and cook over low heat until the flavors meld, 5 minutes.

4. Add the lobsters and stir to coat them evenly in the mixture. Increase the heat to medium. Pour in the wine, stirring to combine, and cook until the wine has evaporated and the lobster is cooked, about 5 minutes. Season with salt and pepper to taste.

5. Add the pasta and pepper flakes to the mixture and stir to distribute the pasta evenly so it doesn't stick together. Stir in the remaining 3 cups / 750 ml hot water and cook until the pasta is al dente, 6 minutes (or according to the package directions). Taste and season with more salt and pepper if needed. Remove the pan from the heat.

6. Serve immediately, garnished with extra basil leaves and a drizzle of olive oil, if desired.

LOBSTER SOUFFLÉ

One Christmas we were all watching an Agatha Christie miniseries, *And Then There Were None,* as we always do around the holidays. It's a very aesthetic production, a bit gloomy but beautiful, and one night all the guests on Soldier Island are fed a lobster soufflé. I couldn't stop thinking of the soufflé—I think I dreamed of it for two days until I just made one myself. I didn't have the recipe from the show; I just made it up, and it's incredibly tasty, old-fashioned, and elegant in that rustic type of way. Now it's a Christmas staple.

3½ tablespoons / 50 g unsalted butter, plus more for greasing the ramekins

6 tablespoons / 50 g all-purpose flour, plus more for dusting

½ cup / 120 ml whole milk

1¼ cups / 300 ml store-bought lobster bisque

6 large eggs, separated

½ cup / 50 g grated Parmigiano Reggiano cheese

1 teaspoon fine sea salt

1 teaspoon freshly ground black pepper

1 pound/ 500 g lobster meat, chopped into bite-size pieces

SERVES 6

1. Preheat the oven to 400°F / 200°C. Grease six soufflé ramekins (6 ounces / 180 ml each) with butter and dust with flour, shaking out any excess. Place the molds in the freezer until ready to use.

2. In a medium saucepan, melt the butter over medium heat until it foams. Add the flour and whisk continuously until a paste forms, 2 to 3 minutes. Reduce the heat to low and gradually add the milk and bisque, whisking constantly to prevent lumps. Bring to a simmer over low heat and cook, whisking constantly, until the sauce thickens, about 3 minutes. Remove from the heat and let cool slightly.

3. Once the sauce has cooled slightly, add the egg yolks, one at a time, whisking until fully incorporated after each addition. Stir in the Parmigiano Reggiano and salt and pepper. Gently fold in the lobster meat to evenly distribute.

4. In a large bowl, use a hand mixer with a whisk attachment to beat the egg whites until stiff peaks form. Working in batches, gently fold the egg whites into the lobster mixture.

5. Fill each prepared soufflé mold about two-thirds full. Place the molds on a baking sheet and bake until they are golden brown and puffed, about 20 minutes. Serve immediately.

LA TORTA DI NATALE

Vanilla Chestnut Christmas Cake

I've been making this cake, the oldest entry on the menu, almost since our very first Christmas together. Chestnuts are one of my weaknesses, an all-time favorite taste—as a little girl, I would get my mother to buy me a tube of chestnut paste, and I would take it to school as often as possible. This cake is rich and flavorful, but it's also light as chiffon and airy, which is what you need after all the lobster. Christmas isn't Christmas without this cake.

4 large eggs, separated

5½ tablespoons / 80 g salted butter, at room temperature, plus more for greasing the pan

1 pound / 500 g crème de marron (sweetened vanilla chestnut cream)

½ cup / 55 g self-rising flour, sifted, plus more for dusting

Powdered sugar, for dusting

4 glazed chestnuts (marrons glacés), for garnish (optional)

SERVES 4 TO 6

1. Preheat the oven to 350°F / 180°C. Generously grease a 9-inch / 23 cm cake pan with butter and dust with flour, shaking out any excess.

2. In a large bowl, whisk together the egg yolks, butter, and chestnut cream until smooth. Fold in the sifted flour until fully incorporated.

3. In a separate large bowl, use a hand mixer with a whisk attachment to beat the egg whites until stiff peaks form. Gently fold the whisked egg whites into the chestnut mixture, taking care to maintain the airy texture.

4. Pour the batter into the prepared pan. Bake until the cake is golden brown and a toothpick inserted into the center comes out clean, about 40 minutes. Let cool in the pan for about 10 minutes before unmolding onto a wire rack. Let cool completely.

5. Before serving, dust the cake with powdered sugar and decorate with the glazed chestnuts (if using).

MPARI

ONG.

EPILOGUE

When we lived in Paris, our lives, as they do now, revolved around food. Our family was smaller then—just a few kids, although it seemed like a lot then—and on weekends we'd peruse the markets, plan our dinners, go to our favorite bistros, and usually at some point during the weekend we'd pop into a bookstore, mainly just to browse.

My husband and I both love books, and we'd sometimes imagine what it would be like to walk into a bookstore and find our own creation on the shelves. We didn't know then what kind of book it would be. Photography, maybe travel. A restaurant guide, perhaps. In any case, it was just a little fancy, and we weren't even half serious about it.

Later, when my cooking blog took off and I was offered a book deal, it seemed quite unreal. At that time, I had no plans or ambitions for more books. One already felt very special—something for our grandchildren, I would tell myself, a reminder of their grandmother who loved cooking and an insight into how their parents were brought up.

Maybe one book was enough. Some authors have shelves to their name, but I wasn't sure that was for me.

As it happens, the books have kept coming, organically and in keeping with my life and the food I've been discovering and loving over the years.

I don't think it's a good idea to do a cookbook just for the sake of it (or any book, for that matter). A cookbook needs to exist for a reason. It has to satisfy someone's needs and to inspire their cooking.

If you want to know how to make a Milanese veal cutlet you can just google it, and I'm sure you'll find something decent online. But to look up that recipe, you have to know that it exists in the first place, and you need to be, for some reason, inspired to cook it. I own a large collection of cookbooks. The ones I enjoy most put me in a frame of mind; they connect me with something I want to be a part of. They put recipes in context with someone I like or somewhere I'd like to be. And I trust the recipes and know they'll be delicious.

I hope the recipes in this book will work for you and that at least some of them will become staples in your home. I hope that you have found dishes here that you otherwise might not have found, and that you have learned something new.

ACKNOWLEDGMENTS

I want to express my heartfelt gratitude to my husband for being my soulmate and the exceptional photographer who captures our journey. Big love to you. You are my eternal love.

To my wonderful children, thank you for being little angels and adventurous eaters, filling our mealtimes with joy.

A special thank-you to Rica Allannic for being the driving force behind everything; you are the godmother of all our books.

To Jennifer Sit and the amazing team at Clarkson Potter, your patience and support have been invaluable, and I truly appreciate each of you.

Andrea Ferolla and Daria Reina, you inspire always.

Thank you, Paolo Badesco and Costantino Affuso, for your guidance in bringing our kitchen dreams to life.

A special shout-out to Homewood—you truly set the standard for excellence.

To all my readers, your unwavering support since day one has made this journey possible; it means the world to me.

And to my Italian friends in the restaurant world, your dedication and passion for cooking the best family meals continue to inspire me every single day.

INDEX